WOODEN BOATS & IRON MEN

A World War II Sailor's Life Story and His Passion To Help
Save One of the Last Surviving PT Boats

BY LILLY ROBBINS BROCK

WOODEN BOATS & IRON MEN

Copyright © 2016 Lilly Brock

Official Website: http://www.lillyrobbinsbrock.com

DEDICATION

"All the great things are simple, and many can be expressed in a
single word: freedom, justice, honor, duty, mercy, hope."

~ Winston Churchill

To my father, a World War II veteran, and every other veteran who has
stepped forward to protect and serve our country, the United States of
America.

It will be my honor to donate a portion of the proceeds of the sale of
this book to the nonprofit organization, Save the PT Boat, Inc. Their
mission is to maintain, operate and display the historical relic, PT-658, as
a living memorial to honor the many U.S. sailors who manned these
small wooden warships.

You can visit PT-658 at Pier 307 at Vigor Shipyard, Swan Island,
Portland, Oregon. Entry is through the locked gate 18 opposite Peterbilt

at 5555 North Lagoon Avenue.

Volunteers conduct tours on Monday, Thursday and Saturday between the hours of 9:00 a.m. and 4:00 p.m.

For more details, go to www.savetheptboatinc.com. While you're there, take a virtual tour of the grand lady, PT-658.

TABLE OF CONTENTS

INTRODUCTION

The Discovery

"The world unwraps itself to you, again and again as soon as you are ready to see it anew."

~ Gregory McGuire

One box stood out from the rest. Large black letters marched across the lid spelling out the word *irreplaceable*. We moved into our new house two years ago, and several unopened boxes were relegated to the basement for temporary storage until we could sort through them. If truth were told, it had actually been over thirty years since I'd even glanced at these boxes. I asked myself, "What did I save in this particular box?" I slid my fingers across the now brittle tape. My curiosity was peaked, and my heart skipped a beat as I pulled the strip of tape from the box.

I was pretty sure I would find photos of family. Yes, there were pictures of my parents, grandparents, aunts and uncles. Family members who have all passed on. There were pictures of my siblings and myself as children. Now we're adults, and fortunate to still be among the living. I took a mental trip into the past as I looked at each photo. My journey was filled with both happiness and sadness. I sighed —yes, these photos were irreplaceable.

After surveying each layer of memorabilia, I reached the bottom of the box. A large manila envelope was resting there. It was marked in my handwriting, "Dad, 1943, somewhere on the African battle front." The envelope was sealed with tape. The tape didn't want to release itself as I peeled it away. It was as if it still needed to perform its function. I pulled out two crumpled yellowed letters written by my dad to his brother. I held them close to me for a moment. And as I read them, tears were forming. I brushed them away for fear they might stain the letters. These were something sacred waiting to be rediscovered. I thanked myself for preserving them.

I savored every word in Dad's letters as he described what life was like living in foxholes and eating c-rations.

In some of Dad's words in one of his letters, he wrote:

"What experiences we have gone through here we shall never forget. Two things you learn to do here very good. One is to dig a very deep foxhole. The other is to duck at the right time. One thing about artillery shells is that you can usually hear the whistles before they strike. They remind me of a rattlesnake in that way. They strike swift and deadly. Through it all, you

sorta learn to adjust your living accordingly. We all want to get the job over, the sooner the better. No matter what we go through, we can take it."

I read the words of a young man filled with emotions that only war could stir. Even so, I recognized the personality of the man I knew, my dad. He survived the entire war, and I was born three years later—a Baby Boomer. Because I am a Baby Boomer, I feel a special connection to that *Greatest Generation*--a generation that endured the Depression and World War II.

I'm often surprised these days when I refer to myself as a Baby Boomer, and I'm asked, "What is a Baby Boomer?"

I simply reply, "Imagine all the surviving warriors returning home at the end of the war. What's the result? A huge spike in births."

I regret that I didn't ask Dad more questions about his life on the battlefront. Of course, there were a few stories.

One such story I recall was when Dad was caught behind enemy lines. He had been chosen to be a mail courier and carried the mail from one unit to the next, which he performed successfully many times. But there was one unforgettable day. When he returned to his own unit, he discovered most of the men were killed, and anyone that survived was gone. He was on his own in enemy territory. Then, while searching for an escape route, he came upon a wounded British soldier. Dad did what he could to dress the soldier's wounds, and took him along with him. How were they going to slip past the enemy lines? Since they were surrounded by giant cactus fields, Dad's plan was to use the fields as their avenue of escape. They hid during the daytime in the scorching heat under whatever shade they could find. At night, they crawled on their bellies through the cactus fields. There were times that Dad had to drag the wounded soldier to keep moving. It was a slow and dangerous process. Dad said they had to crawl so close to the German camp that they could hear them speaking German and laughing. After several days of hiding and moving towards the American lines, they finally found refuge. Both Dad and the British soldier survived the war, and the two remained in contact for many years. I still remember the picture that the Brit sent to Dad years later. It was of a young Queen Elizabeth wearing her diamond tiara. The portrait hung on our dining room wall for as long as I can remember.

Dad used to talk about hearing the Scottish bagpipes during the North African campaign. "It was the sweetest sound we could ever hear when we heard the Scots Guards coming," he said. I asked him what the Scots Guards were. He explained that they were a regiment of the Guards Division of the British Army. "They were a welcome sight and sound," he said.

Dad's survival instincts saved his life and his buddies many times, and he was creative in his decisions to control his destiny. He had grown up on a farm and knew how to trap and hunt. I still have one of his old traps. This early way of living combined with his instincts probably saved his life. He was a hero, as is every veteran who stepped forward to serve his country.

According to *The National World War II* website, in their article "Honor: WWII Veteran Statistics", there were sixteen million Americans who served our country in World War II, and now, in 2016, there are just under one million veterans still living (May 2016). I value their loyalty to our country and consider them a national treasure. There's still time to hear their stories, and to honor them.

Dad's letters stirred something in me to seek a veteran who is still with us, and to hear and tell his story. Every veteran has a story. Whose story will I tell?

CHAPTER 1

Finding My Veteran

I was about to find my veteran, but I didn't know it. It was the day for my Daughters of the American Revolution (DAR) meeting. To be a DAR member, each of us must provide documentation proving our lineage to our ancestor who served in the Revolutionary War in 1776. I'm proud of my patriot ancestors and their courage, bravery and sacrifice to fight in the war to secure the existence and freedom of our then young country. I consider them to be the other *Greatest Generation.*

Our DAR chapter is fortunate to be able to use a comfortable meeting room in a beautiful retirement home. Some of our members live in the retirement home. Now that I was on a mission to find my veteran, I realized that I was most likely in the perfect environment to find him.

After our meeting, I happened to assist my DAR sister, Pat, wheel the hospitality cart back to her apartment. On the way, I had to ask. "Pat, are there any World War II veterans living in this building?"

Pat said, "Yes, Maury—just down the hall."

"That's wonderful," I said, "would it be possible for you to introduce me to him?"

Pat told me she would be happy to check with him about an introduction. In fact, she would be seeing him the next day.

The following day my phone rang.

CHAPTER 2

The Meeting

It had only been a day since Pat called me. When she called, she was sitting next to Maury and handed the phone over to him. He and I had a pleasant chat and agreed to get together the next day at his apartment.

I was about to meet my veteran, Maury Hooper, and I was thrilled. As I stepped off the elevator, and walked past the familiar room used for our DAR meetings, I realized that my veteran had been just a few feet away. During the short walk, I wondered if Maury was widowed. It wasn't long before I had my answer. When I arrived at his apartment, I saw a happy scene. Placed to the right of the front door were two dolls—one, an elderly woman, and the other, an elderly man--reposing in a chair. I smiled, and rang the doorbell that I noticed was strategically located to be an easy reach for anyone in a wheelchair. "Thoughtful design," I told myself.

A stately gray-haired man wearing a red plaid shirt answered the door. I introduced myself, and he invited me in. As I entered, he swished the long oxygen line that he was wearing out of my path which seemed to be his only encumbrance. He sat in what was obvious to me, his favorite chair. I took a seat across from him.

I gazed around the room and concluded this apartment was a comfortable haven for Maury and his wife. There was an array of personal pictures lining the mantel, and one special picture hung on the wall above his chair. In one corner of this picture, I saw a portrait of a young sailor dressed in his whites, and in the center, a picture of a motor torpedo boat. Along the matted border were several signatures. "Ah," I told myself, "I need to find out more about this." Before I began the interview, I asked Maury about the picture on the wall. He told me that it was a gift from the current PT-658 crewmembers to thank him for his service and leadership. Each of them had personally signed the picture. Our rapport was comfortable, and I asked, "Maury, do you mind if I use a tape recorder during our interview?"

He told me he was comfortable with the recorder, and that he and his family were excited about me writing a book on his life. In fact, he was well prepared. He pointed to a beautifully bound book sitting on the floor. I would guess it to have been five to six inches thick. The book was the genealogical history of the Hooper family. I was impressed and appreciated the work involved to develop one's ancestral line, and then to compile it all into a book.

Maury told me that he knew I was a DAR member so I would appreciate what he was about to say to me. He continued, and talked about his third great grandfather, Absolum Hooper, who fought in the Revolutionary War. I learned that Absolum joined the Continental Army at the age of thirteen in 1776.

"I feel a special connection to Absolum," Maury said. Then he told me about his own enlistment in 1944 at the age of eighteen to serve in World War II. Maury's voice was filled with pride when he said, "Both of us served in the only two wars in the United States that were declared by Congress."

"I didn't realize that," I said, "but what about World War I?"

"That was an action taken to help our ally, Great Britain."

Through Maury's words, the young Revolutionary soldier was brought to life. Absolum ran away from his widowed mother who was a Tory. During the siege of Savannah, he was hit in his right arm by a musket ball. During the fall of Charleston, he was hit again by a musket ball, but in the left thigh. In one incident, he was taken prisoner, escaped, and fled to Georgia where the Tories captured him. The Tories released Absolum five days later.

Absolum served until the end of the war. A Colonial boy emerged as an American man. Later, the brave soldier received a land grant in North Carolina from the government for his service. He raised his family on that land. The property remains in the Hooper family to this day.

It's hard to imagine what Absolum Hooper endured. His survival secured the continuation of the Hooper lineage. Had he not survived, Maury wouldn't have been born. Anything that would come to pass because of Maury's existence would not have happened.

I understood Maury's connection to that tenacious boy soldier, and the parallel between him and his ancestor—two Hoopers, two declared wars.

About an hour later, Maury's wife, Ima Jo, came into the room, and Maury introduced her. She was charming with her Oklahoma drawl. She positioned herself behind Maury's chair, close enough to lean on it, and stayed there for the remainder of the interview. While Maury continued to talk, every once in a while, Ima Jo caressed her husband's forehead. Such a loving gesture, I thought. I asked them, "How long have you been married?" Maury smiled at Ima Jo, and replied, "It'll be sixty-nine years this year."

Tom Cates presents Maury Hooper with a signed PT crew thank you collage

CHAPTER 3

Journey Into the Unknown

On January 19, 1945, eighteen-year-old Maury Hooper boarded a troop ship. It had been just over three years since Japan attacked Pearl Harbor on Sunday, December 7, 1941, and he was about to be transported several thousand miles away from his Oklahoma homeland to an unknown island in the South Pacific.

Maury and his shipmates couldn't help but be apprehensive. Now the grim reality of war was ahead of them. They knew it had been a long and terrible war. They also knew they might never see home again. While putting on a brave face as they said goodbye to their loved ones, they promised to return. Those staying behind pretended to believe the valiant warriors.

A sense of adventure filled these young men. They were members of an elite group known as PT sailors. To even be considered to become a part of a motor torpedo boat squad, they couldn't weigh more than one hundred thirty-eight pounds, or be taller than 5 feet 8 inches.

Maury knew something about patrol torpedo boats (PT) before he joined the Navy. He had seen the movie "Motor Torpedo Boat" in 1942. He was intrigued about the PT boat; but, after all, he was only sixteen, and being in the war was a distant notion. Nevertheless, the PT boat lingered in his mind. He also knew the decision he would make if he ever had to serve in the military. He would choose the Navy. In those days, there were newsreels about the war appearing before a movie commenced. He immediately recognized the difference between being in the Navy and the Army. Maury said, "In the Army, the men slept on the ground in foxholes, and ate c-rations. In the Navy, I knew I would always have a hot meal and a dry bed."

Becoming a member of this elite team didn't come easily for Maury. But for a twist of fate and this young man's determination, he became one of the chosen few.

CHAPTER 4

Drafted

Maury was in the eleventh grade in high school when he received the draft notice to register to serve in the war. It was 1944, and he had just turned eighteen. "Two weeks later I received a letter from the President saying *welcome*," Maury said. The eighteen year-old Oklahoman had no hesitation about what branch he would serve, and promptly signed up for the Navy.

Basic training took the place of high school, and boot camp in San Diego was to become his new residence. San Diego was a good country mile from his hometown of Tipton, Oklahoma. After going to Oklahoma City for the required physical, Maury and several other men boarded a steam locomotive train headed for San Diego. The accommodations were not what they expected. "Cattle cars," Maury said, "with bunks stacked five high." The train followed Route 66 through the mountain passes. "We nearly froze," he said. Next, the train stopped in Los Angeles where they switched to a passenger train to continue to San Diego. "Definitely an improvement in comfort,"

Maury said.

While at boot camp, Maury was given an IQ test to determine what positions he would be qualified to fill. After he had finished the test, he was called into a meeting, and was asked what he would like to do.

Maury had heard about the new and hottest fighter plane—the P40 Tiger Shark. He wanted to be a fighter pilot, but learned he didn't have the required two years of college. Next, he asked if he could be a radioman. Since he didn't know the Morse code, he wasn't qualified for that either.

The Navy shipped Maury off to the training center in Mississippi to basic engineering school to learn about steam power and refrigeration. He trained for six weeks. Next, he went to diesel engine training where he learned how to operate and repair diesel engines. That training took eight weeks.

With the diesel engine training under his belt, he was now qualified to work on boats powered by diesel engines. One choice was the landing craft vehicle. It was designed with a flat bottom and a ramp that lowered. The design enabled it to transport infantry and vehicles directly to the shore. Maury had heard about the many thousands of casualties during the landing operations on D-Day, which took place earlier that year in June. He thought, *where would I be going when they ship me out of here?* He decided working on a landing craft vehicle wasn't a good choice.

Maury was still trying to make up his mind when he recalled the movie he saw in 1942 about the motor torpedo boats. He knew the PT boats also had diesel engines. That was where he wanted to be--on a motor torpedo boat. He went to talk to the officer of the day to ask about the boat. The officer said there was nothing like that in the military. The three other men standing in the room didn't know anything either. The door happened to be ajar allowing a man standing in the hall to overhear the conversation. The man came into the office and asked if someone was asking about the motor torpedo boat, and said he knew about that vessel. One of the fellows at the barracks told him there had been a draft for twenty men six months prior. Maury was excited and encouraged. He would wait for another draft and sign up.

Two days later, Maury learned of another draft for motor torpedo boat duty. The draft was for twenty men plus an extra two. Maury had to get permission from his CO to sign up. "I want to sign up for motor torpedo boat training," he said. Unfortunately for Maury, he was told they already had twenty-two men signed up. "I was so discouraged."

It was the night before shipping out. Maury and the other guys were ordered to clean the barracks, and to leave them spotless. The entire time, Maury was feeling sorry for himself and wondered what he was going to do. Then the smoke light came on. It was time for the traditional Navy smoke break. He set his mop down, and he and the other guys went out to the deck for a cigarette. Maury was in no mood to be around anyone so he distanced himself away from everyone else and climbed up on the deck rail. He wasn't far from one particular man, nicknamed *brown-noser*, who was bragging to anyone that would listen about being signed up for the motor torpedo boat team.

Maury explained, "In every group, there's always a *brown-noser* close to the commanding officer. We called him that because his nose was so close to--well, you know what I mean. The *brown-noser* was a few feet away from me sitting on the deck rail. The Commanding Officer told him the break was over and to get ready for lights out. *Brown-noser* said, 'F*** you. I'm shipping out for torpedo boat training, and there ain't nothing you can do about it.' The CO's face got white and tensed up. Then his face got dark. He didn't say a word to *brown-noser*. I decided to get out of there."

Maury went back to the barracks and got onto his bunk for lights out. He was still feeling sorry for himself. It hadn't helped to hear *brown-noser* brag about shipping out for torpedo boat training-- something Maury yearned to do. "I laid there on the top bunk thinking about what I was going to do?" Then Maury heard someone coming down the aisle in his direction. It was the CO.

The CO called out Maury's name, "Hooper."

Maury sat up and said, "Over here, sir."

The CO said, "I heard you wanted to sign up for torpedo boat training."

"Yes, sir, but I couldn't get on."

"You overheard my conversation with that sailor out on deck? You heard what he said?"

Maury answered, "Yes, sir."

"He isn't going on the training, you are. I took his name off and put your name on," the CO said, "You ship out tomorrow morning."

Maury was so excited he couldn't sleep. He was up the next morning at 6:00 a.m. with his sea bag packed. He headed to the train to add his sea bag to the stack. He went to chow at 7:00 am and returned to the barracks until it was time to depart. When he arrived, one of the guys warned Maury that *brown-noser* was looking for him, and wanted to kill him. Forewarned, Maury stayed out of sight for about a half hour until it was time to board the steam train. He never saw *brown-noser* again.

"And that's how I got into motor torpedo boats," Maury said, "I will always remember his name, and be thankful for his *potty* mouth."

Fate stepped in, and Maury was leaving Mississippi and on his way to Melville, Rhode Island to train at the Motor Torpedo Boat Squadrons Training Center for thirteen weeks.

CHAPTER 5

Motor Torpedo Boat Training

When Maury arrived at the training center, he knew he belonged there. This was one of the most exciting moments of his life. The PT boat was more than just an image on the big screen in a movie theater. It was real, and it was love at first sight. He was about to become a PT sailor. Maury didn't realize it, but this moment in time would be the beginning of a lifetime connection to the motor torpedo boat for him.

Maury's eyes flashed as he reflected back to that moment. "I was so excited," he said.

For the next thirteen weeks Maury and the other trainees lived in Quonset huts and learned everything about the PT boat. The training center had evolved considerably since the Navy ordered its establishment in 1942. At its inception, there were ten seventy-seven-foot PT boats designated for training. By the time Maury arrived in 1944, the number of boats available for training had more than doubled and consisted of four different designs ranging in lengths of seventy to eighty feet. Maury learned about the unique construction of the boats. They were constructed of plywood, but the hulls were made of two layers of mahogany planking with a layer of airplane fabric that was sandwiched and glued in between the planking. There were two main advantages for using wood as the material for the boats. First, with no idea of when the war would end, every scrap of steel was needed for building the large warships. Secondly, a vessel constructed of wood was light and fast, and the boat could be easily repaired while in the field. If there were bullet holes from enemy fire, the sailors could pull the boats onto the nearest beach and plug the holes. By the time Maury finished his training, he knew how to repair a boat.

The PT boats performed a specific function. They were designed with a flat bottom allowing a shallow draft that enabled the boats to go close to the shore. During training, Maury and his shipmates learned how to maneuver the boat close to the shoreline, and in case of enemy fire, how to zigzag the boat away while activating the smoke screen generator during an escape. They also learned that they would most likely be on their own in such situations. Larger boats would be unable to come close to the shoreline. There might even be times when the PT boats would be used to draw fire from the enemy shore battery by strafing the beaches. The enemy's position would be exposed while a large destroyer lurked in the distance with cannons ready to fire. The boat's best defense was its speed, maneuverability and the use of its smoke screen.

Training was thorough. It was the policy of the training center to use combat veterans as instructors. The seasoned men had valuable insight to offer the trainees. Cross training was mandatory. Since the PT crews were small, it was important for each person to know the other man's job. None of the men knew each other when they arrived at the training center.

Maury said, "The Navy purposely made sure each of us came alone to eliminate any previous attachments."

These men would, however, come to know each other well, and depend on the other while living in tight quarters and carrying out dangerous missions. It was a unique boat, and a special crew.

Maury commented, "In my opinion, the PT boats won the war."

Maury and the other trainees learned that the PT boats played a key role in the naval war. Because the boats were so versatile, they could carry out missions such as rescuing any ship or aircraft survivors, bring supplies to the beachheads or contact guerrilla forces, and escort mine-laying sweeping craft. Another important role was to patrol the waters in the black of night looking for Japanese barges carrying supplies, and after spotting a barge, sneak in with muffled engines, torpedo the barges, and escape. This hit and run operation earned the boats the American nickname of *Mosquito Fleet*, but the Japanese called them *Devil Boats*.

The trainees learned that most of their missions would be done under the cover of darkness. Their fast wooden boat would be heavily armed, and they would each learn to operate every weapon and defense mechanism. Training involved knowing how to operate and maintain the four torpedoes, the two .50-caliber machine guns, two 20mm cannons (later replaced with

40mm Bofars cannons), two depth charges, hand grenades, small arms weaponry, and a smoke screen generator. They also needed to learn everything about navigation and signaling, how to spot ships and aircraft, radio communication, and starting and maintaining the engines.

Maury's previous training on diesel engines at the naval training center in Mississippi landed him the position of Motor Machinist Mate. He learned everything there was to know about the three 1550hp (later boats used 1850hp) Packard motors located in the engine room below deck. There was a starter button for each motor and when the buttons on all three motors were pushed individually in sequence, a loud amplified roar filled the engine room.

"The engine room would get hot, and between the heat and the loud sound of the engines, a man couldn't be down there for more than an hour at a time," Maury said. When Maury climbed up the steel ladder to top deck, he said it took a while for his hearing to readjust.

Once the training was completed, the trainees boarded a steam train transferring them to a naval base in California near the Alameda area. The train made several stops along the way giving the men a chance to stretch their legs and to grab a meal separate from the train. The destination was Camp Shoemaker. The base also included the U.S. Naval Hospital Shoemaker. Adjacent to Camp Shoemaker was Camp Parks that had been established for the Seabees. This arrangement became known as *Fleet City* because of the close proximity of the three Navy service centers.

The trainees slept in Quonset huts once again while they waited to board the next ship that would be taking them to an unknown island in the South Pacific. The war had been raging since 1941. It was now January 1945, and there was no end to the war in sight. These sailors were trained, but young and inexperienced. They were at their last stop before leaving their homeland. Where were they going? Were they coming back? Perhaps this would be a final moment to think about their life thus far, and to wonder what was ahead of them. One thing the men knew for certain—they would be operating motor torpedo boats.

CHAPTER 6

History of the Patrol Torpedo Boat

The motor torpedo boats have an interesting history. After World War I, in 1920, the Eighteenth Amendment to the United States Constitution was passed. It was called the Prohibition Act. The period of 1920 through 1930 was known as the Prohibition era. The Act banned the manufacture, transportation and sale of intoxicating liquors. The ban actually caused more problems than it solved. Crime increased. Smuggling liquor, also known as *rum running*, was rampant on the sea. It became the duty of the newly formed Coast Guard to enforce this new law. The Coast Guard needed smaller and faster patrol boats to patrol the coastal waters. This period did more to accelerate the creation of fast patrol boats than any war or military conflict. The basic design, engineering and construction standards of these early boats provided a foundation for the future of innovative PT boat development.

By the 1930's, the United States was concerned about growing threats from Germany and Japan thereby instilling the need to produce what would become one of the most significant developments for fast combat and rescue boats in United States history. This need would lead to the development of the PT boat.

General Douglas MacArthur needed such a boat to help defend the Philippines in World War II. The PT boat would be fast, versatile, and inexpensive. He submitted a request to President Roosevelt and the military cabinet for two hundred motor torpedo boats for coastal defense in the Philippine Islands.

The Europeans were also aware of the value of the motor torpedo boats. They needed the boats for coastal defense. They began designing PT boats in the early twentieth century.

There are many accounts of PT boats and the PT sailors. Some accounts are known, and some remain untold. PT boats were used in both the European and South Pacific theater of operations. Many people know about the story of PT-109, and the young Lieutenant John F. Kennedy who became the thirty-fifth president of the United States. Surprisingly, I've learned that many people of the younger generation haven't heard the story or the fact that there was a movie about it. As each new generation is born, the gap widens from the history of past generations. History will be lost if it isn't repeated. I feel compelled to narrate a short version of the Kennedy story here for the benefit of those who are not familiar with it should they happen to read this book.

It was August 1, 1943, when eighteen Japanese bombers attacked the PT base at Lumbari Island, one of the Solomon Island group in the South Pacific. The Japanese were on a mission for their destroyers to reach the southern tip of Kolombangara Island to deliver the much-needed war supplies. They knew that the PT boats would be their greatest obstacle. The bombers succeeded in taking out PT-164 and PT-117 that were moored at the dock, and killing two men.

Fifteen PT's were sent out in response to engage the Tokyo Express that was composed of three Japanese transporting destroyers and one escort destroyer, which were heading towards the entrance of the Blackett Strait located south of Kolombangara in the Solomon Islands. The PT's were divided into four sections to confront the four destroyers. Lt. Kennedy on PT-109 was with PT-159, PT-157 and PT-162 comprising one of the four sections.

The PT boats were scattered, and most of them were without radar. Because of the darkness of night and the lack of communication, confusion and inefficiency ruled what was about to happen. One by one, each PT boat fired off all of its torpedoes, and subsequently each headed back to base. Even though thirty torpedoes were fired off that night, there was zero success of hitting the target.

Lt. Kennedy became separated from two of the four PTs in his group. Both PT-159 and PT-157 fired torpedoes on the approaching enemy ships. PT-159 fired off all four torpedoes and went back to base. PT-157 tried to rejoin PT-109 and PT-162, but wasn't able to locate them, and also went back to base. Meanwhile, Kennedy was leading two boats, PT-162 and PT-169, on a southward patrol. They were spread out to form a picket line across the strait. At about 2:30 a.m., a monster destroyer emerged out of the darkness off their starboard bow. At first, Lt. Kennedy and his crew thought it was a PT boat heading towards them. When they realized it was a destroyer, Kennedy attempted to turn the boat to avoid the collision, but it was too late. The destroyer, *Amagiri*, rammed PT-109 at full speed shearing off the starboard aft side of the boat. The boat was literally sliced into two pieces in a matter of seconds. Two of the crewmembers were killed.

The PT-162 commander had seen the destroyer heading towards PT-109, and fired off his torpedoes, but they didn't shoot. He was only one hundred yards away from the destroyer and had to swerve away to avoid colliding with it. The commander of PT-169 was going to fire off his torpedoes but realized he was too close. The destroyer then opened fire forcing PT-169 to retreat and zigzag away leaving a curtain of smoke behind. Then the commander realized there was another destroyer coming towards them from the south. He quickly swung left and fired his last two torpedoes. Both PT-162 and PT-169 turned away from the scene and went back to base. The men on both boats had seen the explosion of PT-109 and the fire, and assumed there were no survivors.

A fire had ignited the fuel floating on the surface of the water, but because the wake of the destroyer moved the firewater away from PT-109, the bow section of the boat didn't catch on fire. The eleven survivors were now in the water. When they realized the bow section was safe from the fire, they climbed back aboard the section that was still afloat. Some of the men were injured and needed help. One man was severely burned. Kennedy and two of the ensigns managed to get the wounded men on board. Fortunately, the watertight compartments had kept the bow section from sinking.

The eleven survivors' refuge lasted through the rest of the night. By morning, however, the bow section started taking on water. They knew it would sink soon and had no choice but to swim towards land. The badly burned man couldn't swim. Lt. Kennedy, who was a strong swimmer as a result of his college days, put the strap of the man's life preserver in his mouth and towed him. They all swam to a small island that was about four miles away. There was an island that was closer, but they feared the Japanese occupied it.

Even though he was exhausted, Lt. Kennedy went back into the water to swim in the Ferguson Passage to look for any PT boats patrolling the area. He saw no PT boats and after a brief stop on an island, returned to the sea to swim back to his men. On his way back, he was caught in a current that swept him backwards which forced him to start all over again. Fatigued, he stopped at another island and rested until dawn before continuing on to his men.

There was very little sustenance on the island they were on so the group decided to swim to another island. The next island was a little larger and offered more brush to hide in, and a more generous supply of coconuts was available to eat. The following morning, Lt. Kennedy and Ensign Ross swam to Cross Island hoping to find anything of use to them. They were cautious and hid in case the Japanese were there. When they determined it was safe, they ventured onto a beach where they spotted a box. They quickly retrieved it and ran back into the brush. The box had Japanese writing written on the side. They opened it and found thirty to forty small bags of crackers and candy. They continued their scavenger hunt and found a one-man canoe and a barrel of water. Then they saw two natives going by in a canoe, and did their best to get their attention. No luck. Even so, they felt fortunate with what they did find.

Since the canoe could hold only one man, Ensign Ross stayed on the island while Lt. Kennedy paddled back to the other men. When he arrived, he was surprised to find the natives he had seen earlier near Cross Island to be there with his men. They proved to be friendly and helpful.

The following day, August 6th, Kennedy and the natives were heading back to Cross Island to meet up with Ensign Ross. Before reaching the island, they came upon him swimming back to the base island.

Soon, a rescue plan was conceived which involved the natives being willing to take a message to the Australian Coastwatcher. Two messages were written. Ensign Thom wrote a penciled message, and Lt. Kennedy carved a message on a green coconut husk. (Lt. Kennedy was able to get the coconut husk back, and many years later, he would keep it as a memento at the White House while he was President). With the aid of the natives and the Australian Coastwatcher, Lt. Kennedy and his men were rescued on August 8th.

CHAPTER 7

The Beginning

Maurice Weldon Hooper was born in 1926, on his mother's 18th birthday, in the small farm town of Tipton, Oklahoma. The quiet town was platted in 1909. It was established to act as a rail line stop for the Wichita Falls and Northwestern Railway. Because of this rail line, Tipton thrived.

Maury was the first of six children born to Ralph and Eula Hooper. His generation is known as the *Silent Generation*-- a generation born after World War I, and too young to join at the beginning of World War II. No one expected a second world war. The designation of World War I did not yet exist--this war was known as the Great War. It was referred to as *the war to end all wars*. Maury was born eight years after the Great War.

Shortly after the Great War, the people of Tipton and others across the nation enjoyed a period of prosperity and social growth. The strong economy gave people a feeling of freedom and independence. The young men who returned home after the Great War were no longer the same men they once were when they left. They had gone through military training and faced and endured the perils of war. Death became a common reality, and they valued every breath of life. These men saw a world outside of their homeland. As a result, they were more worldly and returned with a new perspective that led to new ideas.

Even the people at home changed. While the men were fighting on distant shores, women stepped up and took the jobs that once belonged to men. This shift contributed to women becoming more independent. The women were bolder and changed the way they dressed. They no longer hid their body and even dared to show their legs. Many women learned to smoke cigarettes, and even drank alcohol with male companions in public. People kicked up their heels as they danced the Charleston, and listened to the latest music called *jazz*. This period was known as the *Roaring Twenties*.

In the year of Maury's birth, 1926, Calvin Coolidge was president. Automobiles had been invented, and gasoline was eighteen cents a gallon. Henry Ford announced the forty-hour workweek. The radio had been invented, and a company called NBC debuted with twenty-four radio stations. The writer, Ernest Hemingway, published *The Sun Also Rises,* and the silent film actor, Rudolph Valentino, died. One year later, a man named Lindbergh would fly a plane solo for the first time from New York to France.

The good times for the nation were short lived, however. The tail end of 1929 was the beginning of the Great Depression. The 1930s through the 1940s brought one challenge after another to Americans. Like the Hoopers, the people in the Midwest were severely impacted. The Midwesterners endured a severe drought followed by the Great Dustbowl period. The entire country was in the throes of the Depression that would continue for ten years. By 1940, people were beginning to get back on their feet. Maury and his family suffered through it all and survived. Then, the hammer slammed. World War II was about to happen.

CHAPTER 8

Memories

Maury grew up on his grandfather Hooper's farm in the house his grandfather built. First, his grandfather purchased the small farm, and soon after he bought two more farms. His grandfather also acquired a house in town in 1906. He preferred to live in town and walked to the farm daily where he worked the entire day. Maury said there were times when his grandfather would stay at the farm in a cellar he had set up for himself, and he even cooked down there.

"I smelled the bacon and biscuits coming up from the cellar. Grandpa handed me up a biscuit."

Maury remembered haying time and stacking the hay, and thrashing the seed from alfalfa which they called *farmer's gold*. Oklahoma was also cotton country, and there was always a large crop of cotton on the farm. They grew their own grain to feed the animals, and of course, a large garden for their own food.

Maury said Saturday was traders' day. The community of farmers worked five days for ten hours a day. They got up early Saturday morning, took their Saturday bath, and went to town. The banks opened at noon, and the farmers stood ready for the doors to open so they could withdraw their cash. Saturday was the day they paid their workers. The workers always looked forward to Saturdays.

Grandfather Hooper had four sons, and gave each son eighty acres and a team of mules. There was a house on each parcel. The four families formed a tight family unit. All the cousins grew up together and they always had each other to depend on.

CHAPTER 9

A Lively Child

Maury had a way of causing a ruckus as a child. His parents knew that too well. One day when Maury was just a toddler, his parents took him to a hardware store. Little Maury spotted a tricycle and immediately hopped onto it. As far as he was concerned, it was his. When his parents wanted to leave the store, he refused to get off of the tricycle. He made such a fuss that his parents had to buy the toy and carry him out on it.

In 1929, when Maury was about three and a half years old, his parents were excited about going to see the new *talking* movie that had come to town. By now, the Hoopers had two children. Maury had a little brother who was a year old. His parents took Maury's brother to his grandmother's house since it was located just a few blocks from the theater and took Maury to the movie with them. They entered the theater and found a seat. There was a buzz of excitement. In those days, a piano player filled the theater with music before the movie started. Then the music stopped and the curtains parted to reveal a large screen. It was an MGM movie. MGM always introduced their movies with the image of the head of a large lion roaring before the film began. Little Maury was so frightened of the lion that he started screaming and climbing on top of his mother. For the benefit of everyone else in the theater, his mother had to leave and took him home. To this day, MGM still uses the roaring lion, which provides a vivid reminder for Maury of his first movie experience.

Maury was an active child, and sometimes his brother, Norris, took the brunt of Maury's exuberance.

It was Christmas time in 1929, and Maury's brother received a big red wagon. The two boys were playing on the elevated front porch of the Sears Roebuck house with the wagon and Maury thought it would be a good idea to pull his little brother around in it. Maury tried to turn the wagon by backing it up, but he backed the wagon right over the edge dumping Norris out onto the ground. Unfortunately, during the fall, Norris fell onto a protruding rod that punched a hole into his skull. He recovered, but not without keeping a scar.

"I was severely punished," Maury said.

Maury remembered another incident in 1929, again with his brother. They were playing together. Maury found a monkey wrench and decided to throw it. The wrench found its way to Norris's head.

"There was a lot of blood, and Mother was frantic as she tried to stop the bleeding. She saw Grandpa coming, 'he'll take care of you,' she said. Then Grandpa helped mother dress the wound."

Maury explained that whenever his mother bought groceries, the groceries were bundled in a paper sack that was folded down and tied with string. His mother kept the string and wound it into a ball. On this occasion, his grandfather used the string to tie Maury's hands up.

"I thought he was the meanest old man I ever met," said Maury.

CHAPTER 10

Hardship & Tragedy

It was October 1929 when the stock market crashed. Anyone who had purchased a home, furnishings, appliances, or an automobile on loan lost everything through repossessions. Credit inflation along with increased government spending and over speculation in the stock market caused the crash. Banks started calling in loans. People living in the cities felt the impact first. Unemployment tripled.

"We started hearing folks talk about the stock market going broke, but because we had our farm, we weren't affected at first," Maury said.

People living on farms such as the Hoopers were better off than the people living in the cities. The farmers grew their own food and they still had money coming in from selling their crops. They owned cows that provided milk and beef, and their chickens provided eggs. They never went hungry. The farmers were fine for a while.

"Our life seemed okay," Maury said.

The following year, however, was the beginning of a downward spiral for the Hooper family.

Maury's grandfather bought a new Chevrolet sedan. He decided to take the family on a road trip to Kansas to visit his mother. Everyone was excited. On the day of the trip, the family piled into the new automobile for the road trip. The oldest daughter, Eva, had learned to drive so she drove first. The roads in those days were dirt and in terrible shape. After driving about forty miles on the bumpy rut-filled road, they decided to stop for lunch and take a rest.

When they were ready to continue the trip, one of the younger daughters wanted to drive the car.

"Nellie made such a fuss to drive the car that Grandpa gave in," Maury said.

Everyone climbed back into the car and Nellie got behind the wheel. They were on their way again when suddenly she lost control of the car, and drove into a large rut causing the car to flip over. Everyone and everything in the car was tossed around. Tragically, there was a large water jug in the car, and Grandfather Hooper fell on it hitting his back. The direct impact broke his back, and he died instantly. A happy day turned into a tragic day. Alfred Levi Hooper died at the age of fifty-six.

"The trip killed Grandpa. Nellie paid a terrible price with guilt for what she did," Maury said.

Maury was only four years old when his grandfather died, but he has a vague memory of the wake that took place in his grandfather's home. In those days there were no funeral homes so it was up to the family, friends and neighbors to take care of the funeral arrangements. Maury remembered seeing his grandfather's casket and people filing in to view it as they paid their respects. The wake lasted for several days and people generously brought food to share. During this time before the burial, the body was never left alone. People took turns to sit with it around the clock.

CHAPTER 11

Unexpected Blow

In spite of the tragedy, the Hooper family continued to carry on. Then, in 1932, their life changed. Maury and his family were picking cotton and preparing it to take to town to sell just as they had been doing for the past several years. The Hoopers always had a big crop of cotton. They loaded up the wagon and drove into town. When they arrived, they pulled up their wagon as usual, but it was quiet. There were no buyers, and therefore, no money. It was a devastating and unexpected blow for the family. The rolling momentum of the depression had caught up with them.

"My family was overwhelmed with sadness and despair. I remember them crying. We were without money until 1937," Maury said.

The Hoopers and the other people living in the rural areas did what they could to survive. They continued to grow their gardens, so at least they didn't go hungry. The families also learned to barter with each other and support the other.

But it was a different situation for the people living in the cities. Food was scarce. Many people were left homeless and were forced to stand in breadlines that stretched across blocks. If the charitable organizations hadn't set up soup kitchens, the homeless would have starved. Eventually, the government stepped in to assist. Maury's family felt sorry for the city people. He remembered the hobos on the trains that passed through town. They were a common sight in the rural settlements.

"The hobos would hop off the train and come to our house. Mom would fix them a good meal. It was exciting to hear their stories."

The downhill spiral continued for the Hoopers. That same year, another hardship fell upon the family. Maury's grandmother died. With both grandparents now deceased, the farm fell into the hands of the executrix of the estate, Grandfather Hooper's oldest daughter. This circumstance had a direct impact on Maury and his family. The daughter ordered the family to move off the land. Now they had no money and no home. Like the people in the city, they were homeless.

Maury's father, Ralph, was desperate to find work. After Ralph and his brother had scouted ahead looking for work, Ralph moved his family to Woodward County in northern Oklahoma where he and his brother had found work on a ranch. Their job was to help the rancher move his prime cattle to Colorado. They left the old cattle behind.

Maury said, "We lived on the ranch in a tent with a dirt floor in a pear orchard. I remember eating those green pears. We lived that way for about a year."

Maury told the story about a government man arriving at the ranch. The man rounded up the old cattle and drove them into the barn to be shot. The rancher could no longer provide feed for the cattle and agreed to the arrangement with the government to help feed hungry people. After the cattle had been shot, people came to retrieve one cow per family. Maury, who was six years old at the time, remembered seeing the recipients put a line on the lifeless cow, and drag it to their wagon. Maury's family was allowed to keep one yearling for themselves. There was also one old milk cow. Maury and the other children on the ranch hid her, but the government man counted one cow short. He promptly found the cow and took it to the barn to be shot. Maury and the other children could hear the shots and they were broken hearted.

CHAPTER 12

Drought & the Great Dust Bowl

By 1934 the Hoopers moved back to Tipton, but they still had no permanent place to live. Then, life got even tougher. At the beginning of that year, there were three waves of drought that lasted until the winter of 1940. The impact of the droughts combined with the condition of the land throughout the Midwest resulted in extraordinary devastation. Much of the land was stripped barren by the methods used for crops by farmers in previous years. Because of those farmers' plowing methods, the land was depleted of the former rich soil. The overplowing stripped away the deep-rooted vegetation that helped trap the soil and hold the moisture.

Man had changed the ecology of the land. As a result, the land was left unanchored turning it into dust. The drought, of course, made the conditions worse. The dry heat turned the soil into a fine powdery dust, leaving it easily lifted by the wind. It was the perfect set of conditions for the birth of the *Great Dust Bowl*. This period of time was known as the *Dirty Thirties*.

Many of the Oklahomans were forced to abandon their farms and migrated to California. Now the people living in the Dust Bowl states were suffering from both the Depression and the Dust Bowl. The Oklahomans who migrated were nicknamed *Okies*. The Dust Bowl caused one of the largest migrations in American history within a short span of time. Approximately 3.5 million people moved out of Oklahoma, Arkansas, Missouri, Iowa, Nebraska, Kansas, Texas, Colorado and New Mexico.

The dusty *black blizzard* turned day into night. Oklahoma was one of the hardest hit states. Somehow, Maury's family stuck it out.

Maury said, "The dirt would blow off of the flat Texas land. We had to wear masks outside. We couldn't even see the light in the daytime. We couldn't keep the dust out of the house. The light bulb would be an orange glow."

CHAPTER 13

Just Surviving

For the next two years, Maury and his family were on the move again. The family walked from cotton field to cotton field to find work. The average wage was fifty to seventy-five cents per hundred pounds. An average worker would pick approximately 175 pounds. Maury had started picking cotton at the age of six on his grandfather's farm. Each picker had a pick sack. There was a strap that went over the shoulder, leaving both hands free for picking, and the sack was long enough to drag on the ground behind the picker. The sack was usually made out of burlap.

Picking cotton was hard, arduous work. The bolls that held the cotton had sharp points. It was a painful process for the hands. There were two methods. One method, cotton picking, was to remove the cotton from the boll while still on the vine. The other method was called cotton pulling or bolling. The boll was removed with the cotton still attached. Cotton pulling was easier and faster. The invention of the cotton gin made it possible to use the cotton pulling method. The gin did all the work separating the cotton from its bolls and cleaned the cotton. Maury and his family were cotton pullers. After they had pulled the cotton, they loaded it into a farm wagon that had been driven into the field. The wagon was fitted with sideboards to allow for a full load. Cotton was known as *King Cotton* or *White Gold*.

Maury remembered his brother calling out "We're pulling bolls!" Sometimes they threw them at each other.

"We lived in boxcar houses. If a cotton field was more than a mile away, we moved on. It was a necessary life," said Maury.

Finally, in 1936, Maury's father got a car from his brother—a 1925 Model T. Now they didn't have to walk. By 1938, Maury's father lost the car. His father had a drinking problem and always managed to wreck whatever car they had.

When they ran out of cotton fields to work in, the family moved to one of the farms owned by Ralph's sister and husband who had acquired the land from Maury's grandparents' estate. For a short time, they had a place to live. Then one late evening, that all changed. Ralph's sister and brother-in-law drove up in their Model A Coupe automobile. Ralph had been drinking and went outside to talk to his sister.

"Dad went out to talk to her. She got upset and was screaming. We had to move."

Next, the family moved to Maury's mother's home place. Maury's Aunt Pauline was the Executrix and had been leasing the house out. She was his mother Eula's younger sister and had been living with the Hooper family ever since Maury was born. She had come to help with the baby and ended up staying for many years. To give the family a place to live, his aunt asked the tenant to leave.

The house was a two-room building with a lean-to attached to the back. The lean-to was supposed to function as two bedrooms, but the tenant had gutted it. He used it as a barn for his animals, and it was a mess. There were holes in the floor that had to be repaired to keep the rats out. They used *Prince Albert* tobacco cans to cover the floors by removing the tops and bottoms of the cans and flattening them. Then they nailed the flattened cans over the holes. The walls were made of slatted wood that had large cracks in between which allowed the cold air to rush in. This is where Maury and his siblings slept. Maury remembered the blowing snow.

"Our bed was covered with snow the next morning," he said.

Conditions weren't the best, but thanks to Maury's Aunt Pauline, they at least had a place to live.

Maury adored his Aunt Pauline. She dedicated her life to Maury and his five siblings--his brother, Norris, who was one-and-a-half years younger, three sisters, Macel, Norma, and Judy, and another brother, Randy. Randy was born shortly after Maury was drafted in 1944. Their aunt was the one positive constant in their lives.

"Mom birthed us, but she raised us," Maury said.

Maury remembered a special moment with his aunt. His tenth birthday was coming up and she wanted to make it special. Times were still difficult in 1936. She told Maury that together they were going to pick enough cotton to earn money for two tickets to a movie. It would be Maury's first memorable movie experience.

"The tickets were ten cents each. We each had a nickel for popcorn. We spent a total of thirty cents. The movie was called *Thirteen Hours in The Air*," said Maury.

His aunt stayed with the family until she met someone in 1946. She married and was happy for only three years. Sadly, her husband had an aneurysm and died.

CHAPTER 14

The Flood

By 1940, the Great Depression was coming to an end, and at the same time, the period of living through droughts and dust bowls ended. The Hoopers had stayed in Oklahoma and handled whatever was thrown at them. Once they finally had a home, they kept a garden growing, and over time acquired twenty-six head of cattle including eight milk cows.

"We were doing okay," Maury said.

But the family was about to face another life challenge. In the winter of 1940, there was a big snowstorm. Then came the rains. The river, which was situated through the center of the farm on the property, began to flood, and the farm was literally cut in half.

"The river ran red with the dust. The flood left silt two feet deep. We couldn't grow any crops, but we were still able to grow a garden," Maury said.

Life was easier the following year. Maury smiled when he talked about the earlier part of that year. He was fifteen.

"Now comes the good part of my life," he said.

Located next to their farm was a section of government land that couldn't be fenced. It happened to be good grazing land for their cows.

"It became my lot in life to herd the cows there to graze. Dad bought me an old mule and a riding pony. I had my horse, dog, a .22 caliber rifle and a western love storybook. I sat under the tree reading the book. I was living the good life for about two years."

Maury had a close relationship with his mother. Every Monday was laundry day, and he was always by her side helping her with the laundry. He carried water from a distant windmill that was equipped with a water pump and emptied the water into her pots. Then he split wood so his mother could boil the water in each pot. When she finished the washing process, Maury helped her hang the laundry on the clothesline.

His mother had a rough life living with a husband who had a drinking problem. Maury knew she stayed with him because of her children. "I was always grateful for that," he said.

CHAPTER 15

The European War

The Hooper family and their neighbors were beginning to take control of their lives. They had faced one challenge after another. There was very little communication at that time of what was happening in the world. While they had been fighting their own battles, Europe was in the throngs of war. Germany invaded Poland in 1939. England and France reacted, and declared war on Germany. This was the beginning of what would become World War II. After the invasion of Poland, Germany invaded the Netherlands, Belgium, and Luxembourg. Then they took France. Italy became involved under the fascist dictator Mussolini and declared war on France and England.

In 1940, German warplanes bombed London for fifty-seven nights. The bombings didn't end until the following May of 1941. More than 40,000 people would die during the German blitz. Soon after, Germany, Italy, and Japan signed a treaty known as the Tripartite Pact, making the three countries allies against England and France. The United States had been helping England and France, and they were warned to stop supporting the two countries.

It wasn't long before Hitler made his move and began herding Jewish people into Nazi prison camps. During the Holocaust, six million Jews would be murdered. Germany conquered Greece and Yugoslavia next and moved on to the Soviet Union.

The United States was continuously pulled further into the conflict. In October of 1941, a German submarine torpedoed the U.S. Navy destroyer *Reuben James* in the North Atlantic. It was the first U.S. warship sunk in the European War. Out of one hundred sixty crewmembers, only forty-five survived.

Those Americans who were fortunate enough to possess radios would have been able to listen to the bits and pieces of news about the European War. They might have listened to the *Fireside Chats* of Franklin D. Roosevelt who always spoke directly to the American people as though he was in their living room. In September of 1939 in one of his chats, he told Americans that every effort would be made to keep the United States neutral, and the nation would not enter into the war. He said he believed it wasn't going to happen.

"I have said this before, but I shall say it again and again: your boys are not going to be sent into any foreign wars." Roosevelt, 1940.

CHAPTER 16
Pearl Harbor
December 7, 1941

Maury and his family were out picking cotton in the cotton fields. It was Monday, December 8, 1941. They saw a farmer approaching them. He wore a grim expression, and for good reason--he had shocking news. The Japanese had bombed Pearl Harbor the day before causing massive casualties and destruction. President Roosevelt and Britain were declaring war on Japan. The Hooper family and the people of the nation were huddled around their radios to listen to the president's somber voice as he addressed Americans about the Pearl Harbor attack, calling December 7th "a date which will live in infamy..."

Ralph Hooper was thirty-eight, and, like all eligible men of the nation, had to register for the draft. He wasn't anxious to go and figured it was just a matter of time before he would be called to serve. Nearly a year passed, and he still hadn't been drafted. Then on December 5, 1942, a presidential order changed the age range for the draft from age twenty-one to forty-five to age eighteen to thirty-eight. He considered himself lucky when he turned thirty-nine before he was drafted. Ralph Hooper didn't have to go to war. Maury knew that if the war were still in progress when he turned eighteen, it would be him going in place of his father. He felt duty bound.

The entire country was affected by the war whether it was voluntary or involuntary. Just as they did during World War I, women took the place of men working in factories and defense plants. They learned to be electricians, welders and riveters. The nickname *Rosie the Riveter* was born.

Women also helped with the farming duties. By 1945 in Maury's home state of Oklahoma, approximately 18,500 women worked on the farms. During the European war, there was heavy demand from the American farmers for food. The farmers in Maury's state and the other Plains states benefited from the demand. The Depression slump was disappearing, and they were able to gradually increase their prices. After Pearl Harbor, the demand was even greater for an expanding military. A new phrase was conceived—*food for defense.* As the demand for food increased, the labor shortage increased. The farmers added children to the workforce. Many children, such as Maury, were already accustomed to working in the cotton fields during normal times. Some civic organizations provided volunteers to help the farmers. The farmers experienced a difficult time hiring locals. The locals didn't want to do the backbreaking work on a farm for a wage when they could earn a higher wage in the city. Some farmers resorted to hiring Mexicans. They were referred to as *braceros.*

Because iron and steel were being reserved for the military, the farmers also had to deal with a shortage of farm equipment. If a piece of equipment wore out, the farmer couldn't replace it. He either had to function without it, or borrow it from a neighbor. The farmers were challenged with the massive demand and the labor shortage, but they were proud to be contributing to the war effort.

Life was altered. Food, gas and clothing were rationed. Scrap metal and rubber were collected and recycled to produce armaments.

Americans planted gardens, which became known as *victory* gardens, as an alternative to being limited to rationed food. Ration stamps were issued to families to buy their allotment of everything from meat, sugar, fat, butter, vegetables, fruit, gas, tires, clothing and fuel oil. Those people who lived in the country had the same advantage that they had during the Depression. They could grow most of their own food. If they had chickens, they had eggs. If they had milk cows, and could feed the milk cows, they had milk, cream and cheese.

The radio was the primary source of news and entertainment. With loved ones overseas, Americans at home coveted any news about the fighting. Entertainers such as Bob Hope and his entourage of singers, actors, and comedians performed before thousands of servicemen at the military bases. These programs were aired on the radio for the listeners in the states.

The movies became a popular escape. There was always a ten-minute newsreel featuring accounts of recent battles overseas.

Many people purchased United States war bonds to help pay for the war.

There was a spirit of unity and loyalty. Some people even destroyed any items in their possession that had been made in Japan.

Because of the attack on Pearl Harbor in Hawaii, Americans feared about further attacks on the United States mainland. The Pacific Coast seemed especially vulnerable, and the people who lived there were fearful and lived accordingly.

Americans didn't trust any people born with Japanese heritage. It was a difficult time for Japanese-Americans, especially for those on the West Coast. President Roosevelt signed a law that Japanese-Americans would have to leave their communities and live in relocation (internment) camps. Approximately 120,000 Japanese-Americans were affected. The living conditions were terrible, and they lived like prisoners. In spite of this treatment, many honorable young Japanese-American men fought in the war in Europe. They fought valiantly, and the Japanese-American unit became the most decorated combat unit of its size in Army history.

It was tough for those who had loved ones in the war. Where were they? Were they dead or alive? Would death knock on the door with the delivery of the dreaded Western Union telegram?

CHAPTER 17

School

In spite of the war, the Hoopers continued to live as normally as possible. In 1943, Maury's father purchased a house in town. Maury worked in a grocery store, and his brother worked at a service station.

School was four miles away so the boys rode the bus. During the school years, they were in and out of school. They and other children in the area were expected to work in the cotton fields during harvest season. Maury and his brother had to help bring in an income for the family. If it happened to rain, they could go back to school.

"We were poor people," he said. "Sometimes I would put myself down, but got along well, and was well liked. The nice looking girls that you would like to date went for the jocks. The little poor girls were right there. They liked me."

In prior years before the move to town, Maury went to school in the country. There was a definite contrast between school in the country and school in the city.

When Maury attended eighth grade, he was in a one-room district school with three or four students in a class. He finished eighth grade and got his diploma. His father didn't have any schooling beyond the eighth grade. Maury said, "That's how it was for that generation."

When Maury was ready to start the ninth grade, he had to attend what was called the *higher* school that was located in the city. There he completed the ninth and tenth grade.

In 1944, he started eleventh grade. When he turned eighteen, he received a notice to register for the draft.

Not unexpectedly, his time had come. He raised his right hand and swore to serve his country.

CHAPTER 18

Leaving the Homeland

What would it be like for an eighteen-year-old farm boy to be thrust into a world unlike anything he had ever known? Maury was on a ship that was taking him on a seven-thousand-mile journey across the Pacific Ocean to an unknown location in the South Pacific. He and many of his shipmates had never been aboard a ship. Every sight, sound, smell, and taste would be a new experience. He had already been toughened up by what life had handed him in his short span of life, and he possessed a profound sense of determination and patriotism. He was ready to serve his country.

He could feel the movement of the ship as it cut through the water and he could hear the lapping white-capped waves against the hull while the shores of home faded behind him. For the next several days, Maury was surrounded by endless miles of blue-green ocean. A stark contrast to the grassy plains of Oklahoma. Watching the sun set over the vast ocean was like nothing many of the sailors had seen before, except possibly, on a movie theater screen. At night the moonlight illuminated the ship's phosphorescent trail. It was a beautiful sight, but dangerous--enemy aircraft or ships could easily detect the white phosphorescent wake.

It took a few days for many of the newbie sailors to get their sea legs. The constant rocking motion of the ship made it difficult to walk, and some of the sailors found themselves heaving over the railing as they suffered from seasickness for the first time in their lives. And, depending on how rough the sea got, rolling out of one's narrow bunk was a definite possibility.

The sleeping quarters were crowded, not unlike sardines packed into a tin. The bunks were stacked at least five or six high, one on top of the other. The quarters were a long way down the ladders into the ship, and they were hot and stuffy. The sailors found themselves spending as little time there as possible. Consequently, the deck was always crowded.

The closer they got to their destination and the nearer they sailed to the Equator, the hotter it became. Sleeping below deck was unbearable. The sailors preferred sleeping on the hard steel slab of the deck rather than spending any time below. Crossing the Equator meant that they were in the Domain of Neptunus Rex. A sea legend from old sailing days called for the Navy men to initiate any sailor who had never crossed the Equator. There were no exceptions for King Neptune. Even the officers had to receive the initiation. They started out as Pollywogs until they crossed, then they became Shellbacks. Each Shellback received a certificate.

As the ship moved east, it crossed over the International Date Line that lies on the 180-degree line of longitude in the middle of the Pacific Ocean. After crossing the date line, they automatically became members of the Royal Order of the Dragon.

Maury said, "We lost a day. I almost lost my nineteenth birthday."

A few days later, they saw the first sight of land since leaving their homeland. The ship passed the Horn Island group, the Solomon Islands and Bougainville.

The battle on Bougainville was still in progress. The Japanese had invaded the Australian Mandated Territory of Bougainville in 1942. They remained in control until the United States landed in November of 1943 to regain control of the Southwest Pacific area. The Australians arrived a year later to relieve the Americans. This battle was considered to be one of the most successful campaigns of the war. The Japanese were cut off from their important naval and air base at Rabul, and airstrips for the US could be constructed on the island.

Much of the fighting was done in the swamps and humid jungle. It was slow and harrowing. While it was difficult and dangerous for the American and Australian infantry, it was worse for the Japanese. They were cut off from their supplies, and they were starving. Some were desperate enough to resort to cannibalism. The battle of Bougainville came to an end in August 1945 with the Japanese surrendering on August 15th.

When the Americans had landed on the island in 1943, there were an estimated 45,000 to 65,000 Japanese troops occupying the island. At the time of the Japanese surrender, there were approximately 23,500 Japanese soldiers remaining. The death toll for the Japanese was approximately 18,500 to 21,500. Several thousand Japanese soldiers died from malnutrition and disease. In contrast, approximately 727 Americans and 516 Aussie's were killed. During the entire campaign on the island, there were an estimated 144,000 Americans and 30,000 Australians fighting the Japanese.

Passing by the blood stained battle zone was a jolt of reality for Maury and his shipmates. Indeed, they were in enemy waters. Next, the ship approached the Admiralty Islands. The islands are 200 miles off of the northern coast of New Guinea and two degrees below the Equator. This area marked the furthest point of the Allied advance into enemy waters.

Island X was ahead. At first sight, it looked like a giant mushroom cap of green foliage. The volcanic island was covered in rugged jungles and a variety of towering palms. A rugged 2,355-foot mountain range ran its length, and numerous rivers and streams flowed out of the mountains into the Coastal Plains. The coastline was lined with coral reefs, and a few of the beaches were covered in vegetative growth along the water's edge. The island was approximately fifty-two miles long and twelve miles wide adding up to eight hundred square miles. They were approaching their destination--Manus Island. It was the largest island of the Admiralty Island group.

In April of 1942, the Japanese had established a small base on the island. Then, on May 18, 1944, the United States recaptured the island and the nearby islands from the Japanese. Manus Island and the other islands were clustered in the form of a crescent shape creating a natural harbor, called Seeadler Harbor. The harbor was six miles wide, twenty miles long, and one hundred twenty feet deep. Wharfs and dry docks were built, and it became an ideal haven for the large warships and transporters. The harbor was needed to build up a fleet for the coming actions to invade Japan. Manus Island served as a receiving base and air base, and it became the largest supply base in the Southwest Pacific.

When Maury and his shipmates stepped ashore, it was obvious that a great deal of construction work had been done on the island. First, the combat units of the Army and Navy were present clearing away any remnants of the Japanese garrison. Then the Seabees followed and arrived on the island in 1944. There were still signs of battle everywhere. Enemy dugouts and pillboxes were scattered over the low hills to guard the approaches to the beach. Palm trees were no longer tall and graceful, but shattered and broken from gunfire. There was spent ammunition strewn on the ground from the guns of both sides. The energy of the fight still lingered accompanied by the stench of death. Construction began, and although they didn't have to fire their guns at the enemy, they fought a different kind of battle. They fought against the conditions. There was heavy rain resulting in monsoons, and therefore thick mud, heat, humidity, malaria and dysentery. Their mission was to turn the island into an efficient receiving base combined with tolerable living conditions. After the Seabees had finished their work on Manus, they were transferred at the end of that year to the next island, Los Negros. They left behind an organized and functional base.

The Seabees played an important role in the war. The group was the 140th US Naval Construction Battalion. There was a need for skilled construction units to work on the battlefronts across the shores. The unit was formed and began training in November of 1943 at Camp Peary, Williamsburg, Virginia. Civilian contractors, builders, carpenters, plumbers and electricians enlisted. This was a new kind of soldier. Their second stage of training was at Camp Endicott in Davisville, Rhode Island. Like Maury and the other PT sailors, the Seabees had been transported by train to Camp Shoemaker to wait for embarkation.

CHAPTER 19

Life on Manus Island

Settling into his new jungle home was nothing like Tipton, Oklahoma. The climate was humid and hot, and the rainfall frequent. The annual rainfall exceeded 275 inches a year.

"We were there for thirty-eight days. It rained every day except one or two. In the morning the clouds formed at the top of the volcano, and around 10:00 a.m. there was a downpour," Maury said.

The volcanic soil was reddish-brown that became thick and sticky. Because of the mud, the buildings were erected on coconut log footings that stood two to four feet high. The Seabees had constructed buildings for the mess hall, heads, showers, sickbay, post office, ship's store, and a variety of other buildings. They were especially proud of the arch-shaped church they designed and erected.

Maury and his shipmates checked into their quarters. They soon found out that the rules were the same on the island as they were back at the training camps. The Navy expected the sailors to keep everything clean and tidy. Maury shared a story about an inspection. When he was back at Camp Shoemaker, he was housed with nineteen other men in a Quonset hut. They all developed a friendship and transferred to Manus together. There was a particular guy from Georgia who seemed to be a natural leader and knew how to turn any situation to his advantage. At Camp Shoemaker, the Georgian set them all up into the position of mess servers to the noncommissioned officers. They, along with the cooks and bakers, got to eat the same food as the officers. It was like eating in First Class on an airplane. When they transferred to Manus, the Georgia fellow got them into scullery duty. Once again, they were close to the cooks and bakers.

Every Saturday was a Captain's inspection. The Captain would walk around and check everything they were doing. He tested the water in the five-gallon drums for dishwashing, the cleanliness of the eating trays and utensils, and even the floor.

Maury said, "The Georgia guy followed the Captain around, and poured some food onto the floor. Then he bent down and licked it off the floor to prove how clean the floor was."

They won the Captain's inspection and were given seventy-two hours of leave.

But, what would a sailor do while on leave on a jungle island? There were no public places of entertainment. Family and friends were far away. There was no female companionship. The servicemen found ways to create their own entertainment and recreation. There were card games, swimming, baseball, horseshoes, basketball and volleyball. They sat on coconut logs and watched re-run movies under a tent shelter.

Maury's entertainment was hunting for *cat-eye* shells. His favorite place was a small freshwater stream that flowed down from the mountain into the ocean. There were marine snails that produced a protective shell (operculum) that was in a green spiral shape and had the appearance of cat eyes. The shells were unique and were used to make jewelry.

"I gathered a sack of them. I was going to make jewelry to send home, but they were stolen," Maury said.

The island natives also gathered the shells and made necklaces and bracelets. They were anxious to trade with the service men. The natives called all the men *Joe*. They traded jewelry, deep-sea shells, grass skirts, woodcarvings, and fishing and hunting spears. In return, the natives wanted cigarettes, jackknives, K-rations, pipes, and clothing. The residents prospered with the American presence. Their life was not as easy when the Japanese controlled the island.

Maury had heard that there was cannibalism on the island. The original tribes of New Guinea were headhunters for centuries. Cannibalism on Manus had diminished with the exception of being practiced far in the interior of the island. Maury was relieved to learn that before any of the servicemen stepped foot on the island, the U.S. Navy had developed a friendly relationship with the natives. Several natives worked with the Seabees when they were clearing jungle growth. The natives would cut through the underbrush with their machetes while shouting to scare any poisonous snakes away.

Many of the natives lived on the beach and strategically built their dwellings on top of stilts that were three or four feet high. The one-room houses were made of bamboo stalks and palm leaves with a hole in the center of the ceiling to allow the smoke to escape from their fire. A house was large enough to hold twelve people.

"The island natives were dark skinned with rough features and red hair," said Maury. "There were black workers in the tent next to ours. If any of the natives came near, the blacks would hide in their tent. They were deathly afraid of the natives."

This color of the natives' hair was not their natural color. They used a concoction of herbs to dye their hair red. Some of them retrieved peroxide from the Ship's store and put it on their hair turning it red/orange. The natives also liked to blacken their teeth by using a paste of groundsel and other herbs and applied it to their teeth daily until their teeth turned black.

Maury and the other servicemen left Manus Island with lasting memories of the jungle hills and fauna, the climate, the colorful birds, the coral beaches, and the friendly natives. The servicemen learned to live and work together in an island world that would never have been known to them had they not served their country. Most of the servicemen were young men, and every layer of new experience and knowledge, whether chosen or not, would contribute to the transformation of each one.

CHAPTER 20

Waiting

Even though the war in Europe had ended by April of 1945, the battles in the Pacific arena were still raging. Maury realized he was in a dangerous theater of operations, and he and his shipmates were aware that they could be called into battle at any time. There were many bloody battles going on, and many yet to come. The battle of Leyte Gulf had finally ended the previous year in December of 1944, and it was still fresh in the servicemen's minds. This was considered to have been one of the bloodiest and largest naval battles of the war.

Even prior to the Pearl Harbor attack, President Roosevelt was aware that the expansionistic goal of Japan posed a threat. Concerned, he decided to recall General Douglas MacArthur, who had previously served in World War I, back to active duty to command the U.S. Army Forces in the Far East. Then, on December 8, 1941, literally ten hours after the Pearl Harbor attack, the Japanese obliterated MacArthur's air forces and invaded the Philippines. Although the defenders fought valiantly, it became apparent in March of 1942 that the Philippines would fall to the Japanese army. President

Roosevelt was closely monitoring the situation and ordered MacArthur to evacuate Corregidor. As MacArthur reluctantly fled on March 11th leaving behind his battered and starving troops, he made the famous statement "I shall return." The troops were on their own, and they were well aware of it.

MacArthur, his wife and child, and his senior staff members escaped on the motor torpedo boat, PT-41 to the safety of Australia. It was a dangerous trip through enemy waters. The trip took thirty-five hours and the boat plowed through five hundred eighty miles of rough seas.

The defenders were forced to withdraw to the Bataan Peninsula and the island of Corregidor. They continued to resist the Japanese until their surrender on Bataan on April 3rd and on Corregidor, May 6th. There were 80,000 men taken as prisoners of war who were forced to undertake the brutal and infamous *Bataan Death March*. Thousands of men, who were already weak and malnourished, died under the harsh treatment of their captors.

In October 1944, MacArthur kept his promise to return to the Philippines, and it was the PT-373 that brought him back. When he waded ashore, he made another proclamation that became famous, "I have returned." The brutal battle finally came to an end in December 1944.

During the final stages of the war, the Japanese were desperate and resorted to a weapon based on suicide airplane attacks (Special Attack Units). The Japanese referred to them as Kamikaze *divine wind* attacks. The Japanese soldier believed in the Bushido code—"A Samurai lives in such a way that he is always ready to die." These Special Attack Units caused significant damage and casualties. One of the most incredible innovations of the suicide missions was the use of the twin-engine *Betty* bomber. The concept was to launch rockets from the underside of the plane's wings, but with pilots strapped to them. There was a crude steering system for the pilot to make sure the rocket hit the target. The Japanese term for the rocket was *Ohka* (cherry blossom). The *Betty* bombers were first used in March of 1945. Americans nicknamed these winged bombs *Baka* bombs (for idiot).

Maury and the servicemen had spent over a month on Manus Island waiting to fight the enemy and wondering where they were going next. Then, on April 12, 1945, President Franklyn D. Roosevelt died. Flags at home and overseas were flown at half-mast. The orator of the Fireside Chats who had addressed and strengthened the American people after the Pearl Harbor attack didn't live to witness the end of the war. And now a new leader, Harry S. Truman, had to take the helm.

U.S. forces had invaded Okinawa on April 1st, and they were met with fierce Japanese resistance. Progress to take the island was made not by the mile, but by the inch. It was proving to be a bloodbath. Truman was concerned. How long would this war go on? How much more blood would be spilled? Would the Japanese ever relinquish the battle?

CHAPTER 21

Meeting PT-238

By April 1945, Leyte Gulf was secure. Maury and the other seamen were transferred to the island of Samar. The island was a stark contrast to Manus Island. There were no high mountains or ranges. The terrain was rugged and consisted of porous coral. On higher ground, the coral was mixed with reddish clay. The rainfall was also different than Manus Island. On Samar, it rained about twelve to fifteen inches per month. There were jungles with inhabitants such as monkeys, huge pythons, and an infestation of jungle rats.

The Seabees were already on the island when Maury and the others arrived, but the Seabees still had plenty of work ahead of them. Living on Samar was less hospitable than Manus Island.

Maury said, "Nothing was set up. The chow hall was a tent. Just a field kitchen. It was easy to get dysentery. There was no sanitation. Everyone got sick. The whole base was in sick bay at one time."

As always, Maury seized upon any opportunity to improve his situation. His quasi hut was next door to the Ship's store. He skipped breakfast and went to the store to find something he could eat on his own. He found packages of cheese and crackers, and candy bars that had been made specifically for the South Pacific—they didn't melt. This was his menu for about ten days until the Seabees built the chow hall where eating conditions improved. Maury's stay on Samar turned out to be brief.

The momentum was building toward the invasion of Japan. The Navy increased the volume of supplies and equipment to be ready for action. As each island was secured (known as island hopping), it was mobilized to play a role in the upcoming battles and to function as a receiving base. Maury and his shipmates were transferred once again. It would be their last active wartime transfer. Maury said farewell to Samar and hello to the island of Mindoro. This time, the men boarded a motor torpedo boat to take them to their next destination. It was the seventy-eight-foot long Higgins PT-238. Maury was ecstatic. The last time he boarded a motor torpedo boat was during training in Melville, Rhode Island. From the moment Maury stepped onto the sturdy deck of the motor torpedo boat, he was infatuated with it. While the boat was idle, Maury could hear the lapping of the sea against her sides. Then the three muffled Packard V-12 engines were started, and the smell of the aviation fuel filled the air. As PT-238 pushed off and moved towards her destination, she left a frothy phosphorescent wake behind her, and Maury could feel and taste the salty spray as it touched his face. As the boat sped up to forty-one knots, he could hear a flapping sound, and looked up to see the proud forty-eight- star American flag waving her stars and stripes gallantly in the wind. Maury was where he wanted to be, and he would remain with the PT-238 until the end of the war. This experience was the beginning of his lifelong connection with the motor torpedo boat.

During the battle on the island in December of 1944, the Mindoro guerrillas guided and supported the Allied patrols of the entire island. Many of the Japanese soldiers fled to the mountains and jungle area. The Filipinos hated the Japanese because of the atrocities and massacres thrust upon their people by the Japanese military. It was estimated that the Japanese were responsible for seventy-two large-scale massacres and over 131,000 murders of the Philippine people. If the Filipinos captured a Japanese soldier, they would torture him, and the soldier feared such a fate. He would commit suicide if he thought he would be captured.

Immediately after seizing Mindoro, the United States Army engineers went to work preparing the vital airfields. Two were built within thirteen days. Next they constructed an advance PT base.

The significance of seizing Mindoro was strategic. The United States needed to build airfields that would allow U.S. aircraft to provide direct support for the upcoming Luzon invasion. The use of the airfields combined with the Navy provided an effective blockade for shipping between Japan and Southeast Asia. In addition, the airstrips were necessary for using long-range bombers to provide direct support for the Luzon invasion.

The southwest coast was a desirable location for an airstrip. The coast was low and sandy with some scrub growth, and there was minimal jungle growth. Going inland, there was a gradual rise up to mountains that created an impassable barrier between the east and west coastline. The mountains also had a direct effect on the amount of rainfall to the area. The southwest coast was virtually without rainfall from October through May. If there was no rain, there was no mud. Good news for the Seabees, and good news for the pilots.

Living conditions on Mindoro were better than those on Samar. One of the biggest highlights for the servicemen wherever they were stationed, was the mail. The mail injected new life into the servicemen's spirits. It was the month of July 1945, when Maury received a letter from his brother that would affect the rest of his life. His brother included a picture of his girlfriend in the letter. Maury thought she was the prettiest gal he had ever seen. Her name was Ima Jo. He didn't have to meet her in person to fall in love with her. Cupid shot the arrow and hit its mark.

"She became my pinup girl. I made up my mind that I would marry her when I got back home," Maury said. Maury kept the picture close to his heart. It didn't matter that she was his brother's girlfriend. With the uncertainty of the war, however, there was always the question in his mind-- would he return home? Would he ever meet Ima Jo?

The PT sailors carried out maneuvers on their assigned PT boat as well as performing duties on the base. Everyone felt they were in a pending mode, but they couldn't allow complacency. It was important to stay alert and be ready to go upon command. They waited one day at a time. PT-238 and its crew were prepared for the impending invasion of Japan. Every boat, every ship, every airplane, and every man was prepared.

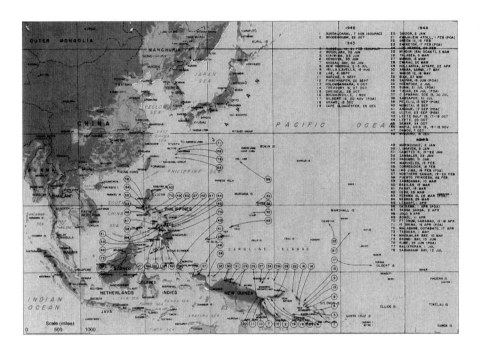

World War II Map of Southwest Pacific

CHAPTER 22

Okinawa & the End of War

In that month of July of 1945, the end of the war was still a big question in everyone's mind. Once the island of Luzon was secured, Okinawa had been planned to be the next step starting in April 1945. After eighty-two brutal and bloodstained days, the Okinawa battle finally ended in June. Once secured, it became the staging area for the U.S. invasion of the Japanese home islands.

It was during the Okinawa battle that the Japanese accelerated their kamikaze campaign. Their new weapon had proven to be successful in the Leyte Gulf battle. The U.S. hadn't seen the last of them. On April 12, 1945 at the beginning of the battle of Okinawa, a *baka* bomb (a human piloted glider bomb) hit the destroyer *USS Mannert L. Abele.* The hit literally lifted the destroyer out of the water and broke it into two pieces. It sank immediately, and eighty-four crewmen died. Ironically, they died on the same day their President, Franklyn D. Roosevelt, died. On another day in the same month, the Task Force-58 crewmen saw the sky filled with 400 Japanese Zeroes heading straight towards them. Kamikaze pilots were flying the planes.

The U.S. reacted immediately, and with the combination of their fighter planes and anti-aircraft guns, they succeeded in shooting down 323 kamikazes. Out of the massive American armada, thirty ships were either sunk or put out of action, and 389 men lost.

By the end of the Okinawa battle, there were over 12,000 American servicemen killed or missing in action, and more than 36,000 wounded. On the Japanese side, there were 70,000 soldiers killed; and unfortunately, approximately 100,000 to 150,000 innocent civilians died in the crossfire.

The capture of Okinawa would pave the way for the invasion of Japan. *Operation Downfall* was scheduled for November 1, 1945, and General Douglas McArthur took full command of the operation. It was to be a two-pronged strategy. The US Army, Navy, Air Force and Marine Corp. would be involved. Both plans had the code name of *X-Day*.

The first prong was called *Operation Olympic*, and the target was the Japanese home island of Kyushu. Okinawa would be the staging area.

The second prong was called *Operation Coronet*. There would be an amphibious attack at Kujikuri on the Boso Peninsula and Hiratsuka at Sagami Bay with additional forces working their way across the Kanto plain toward Tokyo.

While MacArthur was planning the invasion of Japan, President Truman was approving the final act of war—the use of two atomic bombs. The first target was the city of Hiroshima, and the bomb (Little Boy) was dropped on August 6th. Sixteen hours later, President

Truman demanded Japan's surrender with a warning that if they didn't, they "should expect a rain of ruin from the air, the like of which has never been seen on this earth." Japan refused to surrender. Truman kept his promise, and three days later on August 9th, a second bomb (Fat Man) was dropped on the city of Nagasaki. Approximately 140,000 Japanese civilians died immediately or over time from the radiation poisoning. The devastated Japanese leaders had no choice but to surrender. The official surrender took place on the battleship *Missouri* on September 2, 1945.

This final act of the war saved millions of lives. First, there were hundreds of thousands of American, British and Australian prisoners of war who had been imprisoned for over three years and who were living in deplorable conditions. Many of the men had already died. Since some American POW's had been liberated in 1944, there was firsthand knowledge about the terrible living conditions. Second, if the United States continued with the invasion of the home islands of Japan, *Operation Downfall,* it was predicted that approximately one million Americans and ten million Japanese would die. Some estimates reported as high as thirty-five million people would have died.

News of the monumental event became global. Some people heard the news over the radio that the Japanese government asked for peace negotiations. Others heard the news announced over a loud speaker. The news of the surrender spread rapidly. Guns fired and sirens screamed. There was hugging and shouting.

Maury said, "That was one happy day." He and his shipmates were spared the ordeal of actual combat. They were going home.

Back in the states, President Truman announced the life changing news that would bring peace to the world. At the prearranged hour of 7:00 pm on August 14th, he stood in the white house office surrounded by news reporters and proclaimed to the citizens of the United States that Japan had surrendered. People gathered everywhere. Two million people came together in New York Times Square to watch the board on the New York Times tower flash the news about Truman's official announcement that Japan surrendered. The streets were filled with people shouting the good news. Every bar, club, and restaurant were filled with people celebrating. They danced, sang, drank and made toasts. Strangers kissed strangers. Church bells rang. Their boys were coming home. The whole world celebrated. The war was over.

Shortly after the surrender, the PT boats were decommissioned. A total of 121 of the boats were stripped and burned on the beach of Samar.

"That was a sad sight," said Maury. His boat was decommissioned in January 1946. He said goodbye to his beloved PT boat, but he would never forget it.

The boats were intended to be expendable. Because they were made of wood, they were considered to be high maintenance, and, the Navy didn't want them to fall into enemy hands. Some boats were auctioned off to private people with the idea to remodel them into yachts, sightseeing boats and various other functions. There was also a lend-lease program of the boats with the USSR. Some of the boats remained in Russia and some went to Turkey. Four boats ended up in the Republic of Korea.

The Navy announced a discharge points system for demobilization back home.

Maury said, "We got one point for each month served. I needed three more points to get discharged."

Maury spent the remaining three months working as a motor engineer machinist on a sea going tug in the Philippines. After he had earned his three points, he was called into the commander's office. Maury was given a choice to sign over to the regular Navy or go home. He chose home.

Maury was transferred to Japan, now occupied by the U.S., while he waited for a ship to take him home. In the interim, he was assigned to a liberty boat, and ran officers around wherever they wanted to go. He shipped out of Tokyo, and fourteen days later he was in San Francisco. After two years, he was back on American soil and about to be an American civilian again. He left San Francisco to go to Treasure Island, but couldn't find any place to stay. Fortunately, he had an aunt and uncle who lived in Oakland. He stayed with them for the weekend. On Monday, he boarded a train going to Norman, Oklahoma for final discharge. Once in Norman, he hopped on a bus and headed home. When he got off at the bus stop, his father and a friend intercepted his path home and took him to a beer joint. Everyone wanted to buy him a drink, but Maury declined.

"I said, no thanks, I'm going to be with my mom, and I'm not going to have liquor on my breath. When I arrived home, mom had a good home cooked meal fixed up."

CHAPTER 23

After the War

Maury and all the servicemen had something in common with the servicemen of World War I. They came back as different men. They were worldly, more courageous and confident, and ready to take control of their life. The homeland that they knew when they left was also changing. When the men left to serve their country, many of them left behind a life of poverty. Before the war, a third of the homes had no running water, two-fifths of the homes were without flushing toilets, and many homes lacked central heating. Over half of the people who lived on farms such as Maury and his family had no electricity. Like the servicemen, the country would never be the same.

When the war broke out, people unified and put their dreams on hold. Now they were approaching the dawn of peace. Life began to return to normal and the economy was getting stronger. They were carefree, and they were dancing, singing and laughing again. They had hope and soon found themselves in a country that was in a better economic condition than any other country in the world. The American

Dream was becoming a reality.

The world became a better place. Contrary to the belief of the times, the very countries that had been devastated by the war such as Japan, West Germany, France, Italy and Greece, experienced an economic boom. Some referred to it as an *economic miracle*. Japan, the hardest hit because of the two atomic bombs, became the world's second largest economy after the United States by the 1960's. Who could have believed that a long, bloody and brutal war with substantial loss of life could have resulted in such a transformation for the United States and the rest of the world?

Before the war, the birthrate had gone down. When the servicemen came home, the birthrate increased dramatically. The size of the family grew. The GI Bill of Rights was created, and helped servicemen achieve a higher education and the ability to buy a home. Construction of homes increased. It was possible to buy a two-bedroom home with one bath and all the modern amenities for ninety dollars down with a fifty-eight dollar monthly payment.

Maury was settling into Oklahoma life again and making plans for his future. He needed to find a job to help the family. Ima Jo was also on his mind. He had to meet her. It wasn't long before fate gave Maury that opportunity.

His brother, Norris, stopped by one night to go out and have some fun together.

Maury said, "My brother wanted to see if we could find his girlfriend." They found her at a nightspot that had a dance floor. She was dancing the jitterbug. When Maury set eyes on her for the first time in person, he knew in his heart they were meant to be together. *I'm going to marry that girl,* he thought.

Maury found a job working Monday through Friday. Saturday night was reserved for date night. Since he couldn't be with Ima Jo yet, he was dating four other girls. One night when he wasn't on a date, and he was home listening to the Grand Ole Opry on the radio, Maury's brother showed up, and needed help. He was in a fix. His brother had promised another girlfriend besides Ima Jo for a date that night, and asked Maury if he would go on the date with Ima Jo. Maury was more than happy to oblige. He and Ima Jo went to a movie, got a hamburger and a coke, and got to know each other. He asked her out again, and they continued to date on Saturday nights. All was well until Maury found out that Ima Jo was still seeing his brother during the week. Maury gave her a choice--it was either Maury or his brother. She chose Maury, and his brother decided to move on.

Maury and Ima Jo finally together in 1947

CHAPTER 24

The Marriage

It was 1947, and Maury and Ima Jo were getting married. But before they could marry, they each had to wait for their next birthday. Maury had to wait until February to turn twenty-one, and Ima Jo had to wait until May when she would turn eighteen. Finally, in the month of June, they were free to be wed. Oklahoma had a three-day waiting period, but they didn't want to wait one more day so they went across the river to Vernon, Texas to a justice of the peace where there was no waiting period. Ima Jo's sister and brother-in-law stood up for them.

After they were married, they settled in Oklahoma City. Both of them found a job. Ima Jo worked in a five and ten store. She made ten cents an hour. After a short time, they decided that since the pay was so low, she wouldn't work. Maury got a job with Ford Motor Company rebuilding motors. Then he got laid off. His next job was in a general store. Finally, they moved back to Tipton.

Once they were back in Tipton, Maury tried going into business with his brother, Norris. The Navy had issued a $600 certificate to Maury towards purchasing a car, and he had $800 earnings in his pocket. His brother had gone out and purchased a black 1936 convertible and told Maury if he paid half he could have half interest in the car. Maury agreed. The next thing Maury knew, he was forced to pay the full balance on the car because his brother didn't pay his half. Then his brother traded in the car for a flatbed truck because he had an idea how to make money with the local farmers. They followed the plan, and hauled wheat and grain for the farmers and made good money. Everything was going well, until one day Maury discovered that his brother had spent everything they had earned. In just a few short months, Maury was left with nothing.

Maury didn't know what he was going to do next. His uncle had been visiting from the state of Washington and recognized Maury's predicament. The uncle was about to leave to return home when he decided he couldn't leave Maury and Ima Jo behind in such a desperate situation. He told Maury to pack their suitcases. They were going back with him, and he would take care of them until they got on their feet. Maury had fifty-two dollars in his pocket. On November 1, 1947, the newlyweds arrived in Longview, Washington.

Ima Jo was in shock with such short notice that she was leaving the one place she knew as home. The Pacific Northwest was a faraway place, and she wouldn't know anyone.

Ima Jo said, "I cried the entire way. I couldn't stop crying for a long time."

They spent the first week sightseeing and visiting relatives who, until the couple arrived to Longview, once lived several states away. They saw a city that was relatively young and built around the lumber industry. A Kansas City timber baron, Robert Alexander Long, chose the area to build the Long-Bell Lumber Company that he established in 1921. By 1924, the lumber mill was declared to be the largest in the world. Sitting at the convergence of the Cowlitz and Columbia Rivers made the area the ideal location for his mill. The mill was constructed at the Cowlitz River site that gave Mr. Long access to the rail line and deep-water access on the Columbia River.

Robert Long recognized he would be hiring hundreds of workers from outside the area, and they would need a place to live. He immediately began planning and building the city. Longview was noted at that time to be the only city to be planned and built with private funds.

Maury and Ima Jo would shop for groceries and other necessities at the Long-Bell building, later to be named the Merk, on Commerce Street. They would see the beautiful colonial style Monticello Hotel that sat across from the Jefferson Square Park (later named R.A. Long Park). The 5.1-acre park consisted of a plaza, benches and sidewalks. Not far from the park was a beautiful Georgian style building housing the public library. There was a YMCA, and their future children would most likely attend R.A. Long High School. Since Longview was recognized as an important port, they would see seafaring ships sailing on the Columbia River into port to be loaded with lumber products.

Another big company in town was Longview Fibre Company. It was created in 1927 with the concept of utilizing the wood waste that was created from the Long-Bell mill. The company produced Kraft paper and linerboard. It was an ideal collaboration.

Maury and Ima Jo would learn that Oregon was just on the other side of the river, and that they could drive over the custom designed cantilevered toll bridge spanning the Columbia River and land in Rainier, Oregon. The same man who designed the Golden Gate Bridge in San Francisco designed this bridge, and it was tall enough at the center of the span to allow tall clipper ships to sail under. In later years, the tolls were removed, and the bridge was renamed the Lewis and Clark Bridge.

They would stay current with the news by reading the newspaper called the *Longview News*. Maury needed to find a job, and the newspaper was one way to look for a job. He figured he had two choices to apply to for a job —Long-Bell Lumber Company or Longview Fibre Company. He decided to start out with Longview Fibre Company.

On a Monday morning, Maury walked in and applied for a job at Longview Fibre. The man in charge told Maury he didn't have anything available for him, and to try again later. Maury's later was the next day. He asked again and was turned down again. He went back on the third day with his training certificate from the Navy in hand. Once again, he was turned down. Maury didn't give up. He went back and pleaded his case. He told the man he had to have a job. His wife was five months pregnant, he was new in town, and he was living with a relative. The supervisor looked into Maury's determined eyes and couldn't say no again. He gave Maury a job. Maury became a pipe fitter. He worked with pipes that were wrapped with asbestos. In those days, the danger of breathing asbestos wasn't widely known. Damage to the lungs was inevitable. The workers wore no protection. He worked there for thirty-nine years and four months until he retired. Later in life, he would need the assistance of oxygen to breath.

CHAPTER 25

Settled

After three years of renting a place to live, Maury purchased a house in 1950. He and Imo Jo raised their two girls and one boy in this house, and the children lived there until it was time for them to leave their comfy nest.

Maury said, "The girls were Daddy's girls, and the boy was Mamma's boy." Maury and Ima Jo lived there for over sixty years.

Each of the three children brought two children of their own into the world giving Maury and Ima Jo six grandchildren. Sadly, in 1999, they lost one of their granddaughters to cancer at the age of twenty-six. She left behind three small children.

Before their granddaughter died, she said, "I'm not afraid to die, but I don't know where I'll be buried?" Maury immediately went out and purchased three lots in the new cemetery section and told her she would be with them.

He said to her, "You'll have a place to be. You'll be right beside grandma."

As time passed, the Hoopers were blessed with a total of six grandchildren, eleven great grandchildren, and as of 2016, one great great grandchild.

Through the years, Maury and Ima Jo went back to Oklahoma to visit family. In order to feel more comfortable and independent, the Hoopers bought a motor home. At that time, Maury could fill up the sixty-gallon tank of the vehicle for fifty dollars. When gas went up one dollar a gallon, they stopped travelling. They parked the motor home in their back yard to use as guest quarters which worked out well for them.

Maury's next toy was a nineteen-foot fishing boat that he towed to East Texas every year where he enjoyed fishing for largemouth bass. There were three couples--Maury and Ima Jo, Ima Jo's sister and her sister's husband, and a friend with his wife. The three couples fished together in East Texas for twenty years. Maury grew tired of towing his nineteen-foot boat all the way to Texas, so he decided to purchase a fifteen-foot boat that he could leave in Texas in a secure place at their special spot. There is an interesting twist to this little story.

In 1997, both the friend and Ima Jo's sister passed away. The friend's wife and Ima Jo's brother-in-law found love and comfort with the other and married.

Maury said, "Two were gone, but two were still there."

The couples continued their fishing tradition for many more years.

CHAPTER 26

Finding PT-658

Being a United States Navy Veteran is an important part of Maury's life, and he has never lost his passion for the PT boat. He and several other PT sailor veterans have reunited annually since the end of World War II. They meet in a different state every year.

In 1978, thirty PT sailor vets met in Portland, Oregon for their reunion. They started talking about an idea. Why not find a surviving motor torpedo boat and restore it? It wasn't long before they found an old survivor boat that same year, but determined it to be beyond repair. The group didn't discard it, however. They had too much respect for a motor torpedo boat. Instead, they gave the boat to the City of Vancouver in Washington State to use as a historical display.

The years went by, but the idea and passion to find a PT boat never faded. Then in 1992, they learned about a man who purchased a PT boat in 1958 to convert into a yacht. He thought he was going to end up with a very inexpensive yacht. He soon found out that he couldn't afford the 100-octane aviation fuel needed to run the boat. So, he removed the existing engines and put in different engines. To his frustration, the new engines weren't powerful enough to run the boat. He barely made it back to the dock where the boat sat neglected for thirty-five years in Alameda, California. The man died, and his son inherited the boat. The dock owners told the son that he couldn't continue to moor the boat there any longer. With no other location to moor the boat, the son put the boat up for sale.

Maury said, "One of the veterans heard about the boat and contacted the seller. The price tag was $20,000. The veteran told the seller the Veterans group didn't have $20,000. In fact, they didn't even have $200. Four months later, the seller called back, and said, 'If you still want the boat, come and get it. You can have it.'"

PT-658 was rescued.

Every veteran has a story, and PT-658 is no exception.

It was near the end of the war on July 30, 1945 when the motor torpedo boat, the seventy-eight-foot long Higgins PT-658, made her debut. She was one of thirty-six boats contracted by the United States Navy at the Higgins Industries Boatworks in New Orleans. Since PT-658 and her sisters were the last group to be built, they possessed the most advanced design and armaments due to the opportunity of evaluating the performance of their formidable predecessors in the field. She was initially assigned to the Pacific Fleet with Motor Torpedo Boat Squadron 45. With the war coming to an end, the squadron wasn't commissioned, and PT-658 along with eleven other boats, PT-649 through 660, were rescheduled to the Lend-Lease program with

Russia. When the war officially ended, the program was cancelled leaving PT-658 and three sister boats remaining that had not yet been transferred to Russia.

In 1946, PT-658 was reclassified as a Crash Rescue Boat. Later, she was assigned to the Bureau of Aeronautics to be a target towing craft at the Naval Air Facility, at Port Hueneme, California. Finally, in 1958, the proud lady was released from Naval service, and was sold as surplus to the aforementioned private individual in Oakland, California in the Alameda area.

CHAPTER 27

A Lady in Waiting

Since 1958, the valiant PT-658 lady patiently waited to be rescued. She languished in the water by the dock on Treasure Island in the Alameda estuary of San Francisco Bay without any protection, and was exposed to rain, sun, dry rot, and vandalism. Still she hung on.

It was 1992 when the now silver-haired veterans found PT-658. The path to her rescue that began in 1978 finally came to an end. The adventurous group made the rescue official by forming the nonprofit company, *Save the PT Boat, Inc.* When they traveled to Oakland, California to take possession of her, they saw her for the first time. The boat was in terrible condition and looked beyond repair. Much of the wood was rotted, and it was encrusted with moss and barnacles. A daunting task to take on. Could she be repaired and restored? How would they pay for the restoration? They couldn't let her down. She had survived, like they had survived. She was aging as they were aging. She had scars, like many of them. Her spirit rang out to them, and they embraced her. She waited for them, and she belonged to them now.

The veterans flew back home to formulate plans and preparations to move PT-658 to Portland, Oregon. While PT-658 waited for her rescuers to return, she would endure one final blow. A storm developed in the area and broke the boat loose from the dock causing the vessel to run aground on the neighboring jetty. The rocks punched holes into the bottom of the boat causing her to partially sink. Fortunately for PT-658, there was yet another rescuer--the Coast Guard. They saw the boat partially submerged and recognized it to be a PT boat. They immediately pushed it onto a nearby beach and found out whom to contact.

When the PT veterans returned to their boat, they realized they would be making several trips back to California to make the needed repairs before transporting it to Portland. Finally, in the fall of 1994, the day arrived to take the lady to her new home. The veterans were no longer alone in their quest to save the historic survivor.

Many Washington and Oregon people and businesses came together to become a part of saving PT-658. At no charge, the Sause Bros. Ocean Towing of Coos Bay moved the fifty-ton boat from San Francisco to the Columbia River. From there, a unit of the Washington National Guard volunteered their services to transport PT-658 on one of their vessels to the U.S. Army Corps of Engineers dock where it was cradled onto a barge. Foss Towing Co. of Seattle donated its services to tow the boat, cradle, and barge to the Navy dock on Swan Island, located behind the U.S. Navy & Marine Corps Reserve Readiness Center. Numerous other organizations and private individuals stepped forward to assist in this monumental rescue and restoration of a national war relic. On September 4, 2012, the Motor Torpedo Boat PT-658 was listed on the Register of Historic Places. A proud moment for the valiant World War II relic and for those who participated in saving the fierce American-made fighting machine.

At this point, the restoration process moved forward. Over the years, many unpaid volunteers and PT veterans would spend thousands of hours restoring the war lady back to her original splendor. They also worked to raise funds. Much of the wood hull was rotted, and many parts of the boat had to be entirely replaced. The three large 1,850hp Packard V-12 engines had to be rebuilt as well as the electrical system. The volunteers used original PT boat plans, manuals, and photographs to ensure authenticity to every detail. The major restoration process took ten years beginning in 1994.

There was the question of where they could find replacement parts. Many of the PT boats had gone onto the burning pile, while others were dismantled for surplus. The options were scarce. Ironically, the same PT boat, PT-659, that the veterans had found back in 1978 and donated to the City of Vancouver was still in existence. It was sitting in a cradle at Camp Withycombe in Clackamas County, Oregon. The plan was to make PT-659 a museum boat in Vancouver, Washington, but the plan never came to fruition. Even though the sister boat was in terrible shape, some parts were salvageable for PT- 658.

In early 2011, the latter phase of the restoration of equipping PT-658 with a full weaponry armament began. The armament included:

- One 40mm Bofors M3 cannon
- One 37mm Oldsmobile M9 auto-cannon
- Two M4 20mm Oerlikon cannons
- Two twin .50 caliber Browning M2 machine guns
- Four Mk13 aircraft torpedoes
- Two Mark VI depth charges, containing 300 pounds TNT •

Two Mk50 rocket launchers designed for Mark 7 or Mark 10,
five-inch spin stabilized rockets

- One 60mm M2 Mortar: smoothbore, muzzle-loading, high-angle-of-fire weapon with bi-pod, base and sight

The small arms included:

- Two Thompson .45 caliber SMG and two M1A .30 cal Carbine
- Two 1903 Springfield .30-06 Rifles
- Ten .45 caliber Auto Pistols
- One Mk6 Smoke Screens Generator U.S. Navy SO type radar.

And finally, in July 2011, the finishing touch to PT-658 was restoring the paint scheme, Measure-31, Design 20L to the original camouflage pattern. The pattern consists of three shades of green and black. The grand lady was back.

As funds became available, improvements to PT-658 continued. New additions included a new Radar Mast, SO Dome and BN Antenna, spare 20mm Barrel Box, and a life raft with complete survival gear.

PT-658 made her first public appearance in late June of 2004. She was towed to Tomahawk Island Moorage during an Antique & Classic Wooden

Boat Show. She was spectacular. She had gone from a rotting hull of a boat to a gleaming example of what a fierce warship she was meant to be. She was here to stay. The boat was taken on three trial runs during the year. On the third trip in October, three groups of twenty-five people were given the opportunity to board her to experience a thirty-minute excursion on the Willamette River. Her three Packard engines howled while they pushed her to thirty-seven knots (forty-two mph), and her rooster tail was magnificent.

From 2007 through 2008 a boathouse/museum was constructed. The war lady spent many years exposed to the weather, but never again. She is now moored inside a large custom made boathouse where veterans and tourists can see and board her. Visitors have access to over 600 artifacts on the boat. The on-site computer has a database containing thousands of cataloged artifacts, drawings, engine manuals and photos.

As a result of the volunteers and funds contributed, the restored PT-658 is the only fully operational World War II PT boat in the world. This Motor Torpedo Boat represents the spirit and bravery of the PT sailors who manned the PT boats to serve their country. It also represents the spirit, tenacity, unity and generosity of all those involved to preserve this valuable living artifact of American history.

And the giving continues. The volunteer crewmembers continue to maintain, make repairs and run the boat. They are there to educate the tourists who visit, and by appointment and a fee, they will take groups out for a ride on this rare historical World War II PT boat.

PT-658 in terrible disrepair waiting to be rescued

The grand lady is back, fully restored to her former glory

CHAPTER 28

Visiting the Restored PT-658

It was Saturday, March 12, 2016. The day I would meet the grand lady, PT-658. Maury had arranged a private tour of the boat. I picked Maury up at noon in front of his building. My daughter, who is always by my side on my projects, came along with me. We happened to have an out of state house guest at our home and I invited her to come as well. She was thrilled to see a piece of living history.

We arrived just before noon and Maury was already waiting for us out front. I noticed that he was wearing a hat bearing the PT-658 logo, and a navy jacket with a pin attached that had the words *President, PT-658, Maury Hooper.*

We drove south to Portland, Oregon, an hour away. Our final destination was Pier 307, Vigor Shipyard, Swan Island. We arrived at a locked chain link gate. Maury had his key ready and unlocked the padlock. I drove through and parked. Straight ahead was a gangplank that led us to the large boathouse, home to PT-658. Earlier in the day, fifty people had toured the boat. The boathouse was huge, my first clue of how big the boat actually was. At this point, I had only seen pictures of the PT boat and wondered how a crew of twenty men could possibly sleep in the lower section of the boat. It was larger than I had visualized, and every inch of its seventy-eight-foot length was efficiently designed without any wasted space. Seeing this historical boat with all its weaponry took my breath away. Boarding it made me feel as though I had entered a different world.

Anyone remaining on the boat after the earlier tour knew and welcomed Maury with enthusiasm. It was an honor to meet these people and to witness the camaraderie among them. One of Maury's friends arrived with a large package under his arm. He joined us on the deck and told Maury he had something special. He opened the mysterious package revealing a ship's steering wheel. It was the original steering wheel to PT-658. Maury's friend had learned about it being in the possession of the widow of a military man. I asked Maury and his friend to stand together with the wheel, and my daughter snapped a picture of them. The timing of his friend's arrival couldn't have been more perfect.

Maury proceeded to give us a tour of the boat. It was as though he was that PT sailor again. He even moved like a young sailor in spite of being ninety years old. He knew every detail of the boat and the weaponry. By the end of the tour, I acquired a genuine appreciation of the uniqueness of this boat and its crew.

There were two levels of the boat below deck. Below deck is divided into eight watertight compartments separated by built-up plywood bulkheads (walls). The design of these bulkheads made it possible for any door passageways to be watertight when the doors were closed. I was curious about the sleeping quarters that were on the lowest level. A fixed narrow wooden ladder provided the way down. Straight down. I clenched the handrails positioned on each side of the ladder and descended one rung at a time. We were in the forward crews' quarters. Smaller crews' quarters were located in the aft section of the boat that would accommodate four sailors, plus two additional men in the Lazarette (Rudder Room).

There were eight bunks in the forward quarters—four above, and four below. Each bunk had its own pinup girl. There were various uniforms protected in plastic on display hanging in front of the bunks. Maury's uniform was there along with a picture of him as a young sailor and the PT boat he was on, PT-238. Life jackets hung from above. The crews' head was tucked on a sidewall with nothing more than a curtain for privacy. A cook's galley was situated opposite the sleeping area. It consisted of a small stove, stainless steel sink and refrigerator with freezer section. Sitting on top of the refrigerator was an original toaster used during World War II.

We stepped up and ducked through the door opening to visit the Ward Room and Officers' State Room. A watertight door separated this section from the crews' quarters. In the Ward Room, there was a gun rack that held rifles and machine guns. Handguns sat nearby. There was also an ammo closet which once held ammunition.

The Officers' State Room had two bunks complete with a pinup girl picture, an officers' head, a desk, bookshelf, and a settee. There was even a footlocker with personal items near it, and officers' uniforms.

We were ready to go top deck. Maury led the way while climbing the ladder with ease and familiarity. My daughter happened to ask him a question when he was midway up the ladder. He stopped and turned towards her to answer her question. He looked so natural in his pose that in my mind's eye, the image of a nineteen-year-old PT sailor suddenly flashed before me.

Once back on deck, Maury said that we hadn't been to the bow of the boat yet. One of Maury's friends followed us, and snapped a picture of Maury and I. It was a wonderful conclusion to the tour. Then Maury surprised me with an unexpected gift. He presented me with the PT-658 Challenge Coin.

Maury said, "The only other people I have given one to, are Admirals."

I was honored, and it will be one of the highlights of my life. Of course, my daughter snapped a picture of me receiving the coin.

Maury and Lilly

Maury presenting the PT-658 Challenge Coin

The PT-658 Challenge Coin

CHAPTER 29

The Honor Flight Tour

The following month, April of 2016, Maury participated in the Honor Flight tour to visit the World War II Memorial in Washington, D.C. He felt honored that his application was accepted by the Honor Flight Network, and was thrilled to be given the opportunity to visit the Memorial. Maury's trip was entirely paid by the group. They did have one requirement, however. They wanted to make sure that no veteran went alone, and therefore required each veteran to be accompanied by a guardian. There was a charge for the guardian. Maury chose his grandson to go with him.

The generosity towards Maury actually began with the group, *Save the PT Boat*, of which he is a member. First, they submitted an application to the Honor Flight group on Maury's behalf, and additionally they paid the cost for Maury's grandson.

The Memorial was completed and dedicated in May of 2004. Throngs of veterans come every year to visit the Memorial. For many veterans, such a visit is a financial impossibility and because of their age, too physically difficult to complete such a trip on their own. It would be a dream come true for World

War II veterans who are still living to be able to visit the Memorial.

The Honor Flight Group has made it possible for thousands of veterans to visit the Memorial free of charge. The program was the brainchild of one man, Retired Air Force Captain Earl Morse. Because of his efforts, the first Honor Flight tour began in May 2005 with six small planes holding twelve World War II veterans flying out of Springfield, Ohio. As the word spread through the years, people and companies across America stepped up. The nonprofit organization grew from one caring man, then a handful of caring men, to a national organization. I couldn't describe this group any better than quoting directly from their site, www.honorflight.org. "Our Mission: To Transport American Veterans to Washington, D.C. to visit those memorials dedicated to honor the services and sacrifices of themselves and their friends."

I have always held an affection towards our veterans beginning with my dad. My experience with Maury has led me to untapped awareness of people coming together in so many ways to honor our veterans. The PT-658 restoration, for example, grew from a handful of dedicated World War II veterans to veterans of other wars to private citizens who chose to unite to honor their service and sacrifice to our country.

The veterans bring out the best of people. It's been a rewarding experience to witness such generosity and dedication.

*Maury Hooper on the Honor Flight Tour to visit the World War II
Memorial with the Southwest Pacific Memorial in the background*

*The group of World War II veterans on the Honor Flight Tour
visiting the World War II Memorial.*

EPILOGUE

This Day in 2016

Currently, Maury and Ima Jo live in a pleasant retirement community in Longview, Washington. They are surrounded by their loving children, grandchildren, great- grandchildren and one great-great grandchild as well as friends.

Maury was proud to tell me about his great-grandson, Eric, who has the same middle name of Weldon, and has followed in Maury's footsteps to serve in the Navy.

Eric's mother Lori said, "When Grandpa first took Eric to the PT boat and when he saw firsthand what Grandpa did in the server, that's when he wanted to go into the Navy." Eric was nine years old at the time.

Maury, who is the oldest of all of his siblings, is ironically very close to his youngest brother who happened to be born while Maury was in the service.

Beyond family and friends, the PT-658 organization is still an important part of Maury's life, and he has a special relationship with the members and anyone connected to PT-658.

It has been my honor to meet Maury and learn about his life. He is part of the *Greatest Generation*—a generation of ordinary people who were extraordinary. Through Maury's voice I was transported into the 1930's to Oklahoma after World War I and before World War II. I, of course have perspective, because it is 2016 at this moment, and I have every comfort I desire. I visualized myself following Maury into the cotton fields to pick cotton. It was hot and dry, and my hands were covered with cuts and bloodied. Living through the draught was miserable. I was hot and sweaty, and getting a nice shower was nonexistent. Then there was the Great Dust Bowl. You can't breathe and wearing a bandana for a mask is a must. The sky is black, the house is filled with dust, and the hanging light bulb is orange. We're hungry since the gardens and crops have been destroyed. We're thirsty, but water needs to be rationed. After the dust storm passes, life continues and crops and gardens are replanted. There is some food again—just in time for the Great Depression. Life spirals downhill but the spirit stays strong. We either cave in to the difficult times or cease to exist. Then our country is attacked at Pearl Harbor, and we are thrust into World War II. I witness proud valiant people, like Maury, who do not hesitate to step up to serve their country. I see people on the home front sacrificing and doing their share. All ordinary people who became extraordinary, and it is because of extraordinary people that we live in this extraordinary country—the United States of America.

Maury with his great grandson, at the age of 9, on PT-658. It was on this day, Eric chose to follow in his great grandfather's footsteps to serve in the U. S. Navy

Maury as a young man in his Navy whites, 1945 (left) and
Eric, grown up wearing his Navy whites, 2014 (right)

Maury, Eric and Ima Jo

ABOUT THE AUTHOR

Lilly Robbins Brock was born and raised in Olympia, Washington. Her pioneer family immigrated to Olympia from New England in the 1860's. She met and married her husband, Phil in 1968. They raised two daughters who are now beautiful young women. She started her interior design business in 1980 that has been going strong up to the present. Now she and her husband are ready to enjoy retirement and have moved from a busy Olympia suburb to living a quiet life in the country in Cathlamet, Washington on the Columbia River.

Living in the country is the perfect environment for Lilly to pursue her lifelong passion to write. She loves history and has written a historical fiction novel about a family in the 1850's traveling on a paddle wheel steamship from New York crossing the Atlantic Ocean to the Pacific Ocean. Their final destination was the rugged Pacific Northwest.

Lilly is also hooked on genealogy and is a member of the Daughters of The American Revolution. She feels a strong connection to our veterans. Her father was a World War II veteran who fought in North Africa and Italy. When she found two of his letters that he wrote while on the battlefront, she was inspired to find a World War II veteran who is still living. She found her veteran and wrote this book to honor him and all veterans. Consequently, her historical fiction novel is waiting in the wings to be published.

To stay tuned in to current and upcoming projects, feel free to visit *www.lillyrobbinsbrock.com.*

Thank you for reading this book. If you enjoyed this book, please consider leaving a short review on Amazon.com.

ACKNOWLEDGEMENTS

First and foremost, I would like to thank World War II veteran Maury Hooper for granting me the opportunity to write about his life. He was always well prepared for each interview session as we walked through his life. During the process, I met his wife, Ima Jo, who was so gracious to share her husband's time with me, and I thank her. It has been a pleasure getting to know both of them.

I'm grateful to Maury's daughter, Linda, for her assistance, and also his granddaughter, Lori, who provided me with several of the photos used in this book. Lori became an invaluable contact.

Thank you to Wally Boeger, Webmaster for Save the PT Boat, Inc. for answering my many questions and providing photos of PT-658 and other related pictures. I would also like to acknowledge that the Save the PT Boat website provided a wealth of information on PT-658 which I used in this book.

Thank you to Daniel Rhodes, Scuba Dan, dan6454@aol.com, for his generosity to allow me to use one of his photos of PT-658 for the cover of this book. He refers to himself as "an amateur underwater photographer who shoots above water to improve his skills with the camera."

I especially want to thank Patricia Devin who was responsible for connecting Maury and I. She has been very supportive during this project and was even an early reader of this book. Her response was everything an author would like to hear.

My immediate family deserves a big thank you for their support and patience, and putting up with my lack of attentiveness in their presence. My daughters, Alecia and Vivi Anne, my husband Phil, and my sister June, were early readers and proofreaders. Their assistance is truly appreciated.

Thank you to my excellent editor, Courtney Cannon, owner of Fiction-Atlas Copy Editing and Cover Design. She was thorough and on schedule.

A thank you goes to my sister-in-law, Merrily Graham, for her valuable input and support as well.

And finally, I thank my daughter Vivi Anne once again for working by my side as usual. She designed and created the cover as well as formatting this book. It's hard to imagine what I would do without her.

REFERENCES

Following is a list of many of the resources frequently used in my historical research projects which also contributed to this book.

"American History: 'Roaring Twenties' a Time of Economic and Social Change (VOA Special English 2006-06-07)." N.p., n.d. Web. 15 June 2016.

Boundless. "The New Era." *Boundless* (2016): n. pag. *www.boundless.com*. Web. 20 June 2016. The New Era.

Bulkley, Robert J, United States, and Naval History Division. *At Close Quarters: PT Boats in the United States Navy*. Washington, D.C.: Naval History Division : [For sale by the Supt. of Docs., U.S. G.P.O., 1962. Print.

Campbell, Emma. "Bougainville's Hard Slog | Australian War Memorial." *Australian War Memorial*. N.p., 28 May 2012. Web. 22 May 2016.

Center for History and New Media. "Zotero Quick Start Guide." N.p., n.d. Web.

C. Peter Chen (contributor). "Preparations for Invasion of Japan." *WW2DB*. N.p., n.d. Web. 22 May 2016.

Daryl C. Mcclary. "HistoryLink.org- the Free Online Encyclopedia of Washington State History." Essay 8560. *Longview--Thumbnail History, Essay 8560*. N.p., 2 July 2008. Web. 20 June 2016.

"Digital History." N.p., 2016. Web. 22 May 2016.

Finn J.D. John. "Oregon Is Home of World's Only World War II-Era PT Boat | Offbeat Oregon History | #ORhistory." Blog. N.p., 19 Jan. 2014. Web. 5 Mar. 2016.

"Francis Pike - Author of Hirohito's War and Empires At War." *Francis Pike*. N.p., n.d. Web. 22 May 2016.

Gene Kirkland. "PT KING - PT Boat Books - U.S. Navy PT Boats of World War II - PT 109." N.p., 2013 2002. Web. 20 June 2016.

History.com, Staff. "PT-109 Sinks; Lieutenant Kennedy Is Instrumental in Saving Crew - Aug 01, 1943." *HISTORY.com*. N.p., n.d. Web. 22 May 2016.

"Honoring Our Veterans | Honor Flight Network." Blog. N.p., n.d. Web. 20 June 2016.

"HyperWar: Building the Navy's Bases in World War II [Chapter 29]." N.p., n.d. Web. 22 May 2016.

Lewis, Rob, and Wolf, Sam. "The FReeper Foxhole Remembers the Mosquito Fleet (PT Boats) - Aug. 22, 2005." Forum. N.p., 22 Aug. 2005. Web. 22 May 2016.

LLC, Revolvy. "'USS Mannert L. Abele' on Revolvy.com." N.p., n.d. Web. 11 Mar. 2016.

"Melville, Rhode Island." *PT Boat Red*. N.p., 19 May 2011. Web. 17 Apr. 2016.

Moore, David. "Pollywog or Shellback: The Navy's Line Crossing Ceremony Revealed." Blog. *Veterans United Network*. N.p., 25 Mar. 2013. Web. 22 May 2016.

"Naval Construction Battalion Center Gulfport." *Mlitary Bases, US*. N.p., n.d. Web. 20 June 2016.

"Oklahoma Route 66." N.p., 2003. Web. 20 June 2016.

"Operation Downfall - History Learning Site." History Learning Site. N.p., 19

    May 2015. Web. 20 June 2016.

"Patrol and Rescue Boats on Puget Sound." N.p., n.d. Web.

"PT-Class Motor Torpedo Boat." *WW2DB*. N.p., n.d. Web.

"Save The PT Boat, Inc. PT658 Heritage." N.p., n.d. Web.

shannen.bradley. "US Entry and Alliance." History network. *HISTORY*. N.p., 3

    Apr. 2014. Web. 20 June 2016.

Smith, Donna Y. "Tipton | Encyclopedia of Oklahoma History and Culture."

    Encyclopedia. *Tipton*. N.p., n.d. Web. 22 May 2016.

Staunton, Anthony. "Bougainville, One of the Last Dirty Fights." *Unofficial

    history of the Australian & New Zealand Amed Servicesd*. N.p., 2002.

    Web. 15 May 2016.

Taylor, Nick. "The Great Depression." *The New York Times*. N.p., n.d. Web. 22

    May 2016.

"The Atomic Bombs Saved 35 Million Lives." *LEADING MALAYSIAN

    NEOCON*. N.p., 27 May 2008. Web. 17 May 2016.

The CBMU No. 621 Manus-Script, 1944 - 1945. U.S. Navy Seabee Museum.

    Print.

"The Columbia River - Lewis and Clark Bridge." Columbia River website. N.p.,

    Sept. 2011. Web. 20 June 2016.

"The Dust Bowl of Oklahoma." Library of Congress. *America's Story*. N.p., n.d.

    Web. 22 May 2016.

"The Higgins Boat." article. N.p., n.d. Web. 20 June 2016.

"The National WWII Museum | New Orleans: Honor: WWII Veterans

    Statistics." N.p., n.d. Web.

"The U.S. Home Front During World War II - World War II - HISTORY.com."

history network. N.p., n.d. Web. 20 June 2016.

United States, Navy, and 140th Construction Battalion. *Down Atabrine Alley with the 140th Seabees.* Baton Rouge, LA: Army & Navy Pictorial Pub., 1945. Print.

"USS Mannert L. Abele (DD 733)." N.p., n.d. Web. 22 May 2016.

Weiser-Alexander, Kathy. "Dust Bowl Days or the 'Dirty Thirties.'" on-line magazine. *Legends of America.* N.p., to present 2003. Web.

"WGBH American Experience . Victory in the Pacific | PBS." *American Experience.* N.p., n.d. Web.

"What Happened in 1926 Including Pop Culture, Technology and Events." *The Making of a Nation.* N.p., n.d. Web. 22 May 2016.

"World War II Timeline - Remembering Pearl Harbor @ Nationalgeographic.com." on-line magazine. *Remembering Pearl Harbor.* N.p., present 2001. Web.